NIETZSCHE AND THE CLINIC

NIETZSCHE AND THE CLINIC
Psychoanalysis, Philosophy, Metaphysics

Jared Russell

KARNAC

First published in 2017 by
Karnac Books Ltd
118 Finchley Road
London NW3 5HT

British Library Cataloguing in Publication Data

A C.I.P. for this book is available from the British Library

ISBN-13: 978-1-78220-489-3

Typeset by V Publishing Solutions Pvt Ltd., Chennai, India

Printed in Great Britain by TJ International Ltd, Padstow, Cornwall

www.karnacbooks.com

For my mother, Pamela, in loving memory

CONTENTS

ACKNOWLEDGEMENTS

I am thankful for conversations with my distinguished colleagues Maria Cristina Aguirre, Josefina Ayerza, Elizabeth Cutter-Evert, Susan Finkelstein, Janet Fisher, Russell Grigg, Joan Hoffenberg, Brian Kloppenberg, Masha Mimran, Dmitri Nikulin, Carlos Padrón, Aaron Thaler, and Neal Vorus. I am particularly indebted to Eric Anders for his encouragement both as a colleague and as a friend. Jamieson Webster was invaluable in helping me to bring the original manuscript to publication. Rebecca Wallance was kind enough to prepare the index.

Alan Bass has been supportive of my development for a very long time, and for that I am inexpressibly grateful. I have tried here to disseminate to a wider audience much of what I have learned from him.

Norbert Freedman's boundless generosity, keen clinical acumen, and unparalleled commitment to the profession have marked me, as so many others, very deeply. Above all else, I admired him for his strength.

The greatest debt of gratitude I owe, of course, is to the many patients, students, and supervisees that I have been fortunate enough to have worked with over the years.

* * *

An earlier version of Chapter Three appeared as, "*L'effet c'est toi*: Projective identification from Nietzsche to Klein," in *American Imago*, 70, 4 (*Winter 2013*): 563–583, reprinted with permission by Johns Hopkins University Press (© 2013 Johns Hopkins University Press). An earlier version of Chapter Four appeared as, "There is no such thing as transference," in *The Undecidable Unconscious: A Journal of Deconstruction and Psychoanalysis*, 1: 9–29, with permission from the University of Nebraska Press (© 2015 University of Nebraska Press). Permission from the publishers to reprint this material is greatly appreciated.

Unless otherwise noted, italicized emphases in all quotations from Nietzsche's texts are his (or his editors') own. With regard to other authors quoted, I have indicated either the author's emphases or my own modifications.

Clinical examples represent composite and disguised material designed to protect patients' anonymity. No reference to singular individuals is implied.

ABOUT THE AUTHOR

Jared Russell is a psychoanalyst in private practice in New York City. He received his PhD in philosophy from The New School for Social Research, while undergoing analytic training at The Institute for Psychoanalytic Training and Research (IPTAR), where he is now a faculty member and clinical supervisor. A fellow of the International Psychoanalytical Association, he is Managing Editor of *The Undecidable Unconscious: A Journal of Deconstruction and Psychoanalysis* (University of Nebraska Press), and co-editor, with Steven Ellman, of IPTAR's Psycho-analytic Books Series.

PREFACE

What follows is decidedly a hybrid. Devoted for the most part to an examination of texts that belong to the history of philosophy, it promises to illuminate the domain of the psychoanalytic clinic. Today there is no shortage of books that reflect on psychoanalysis from a philosophical lens, and there is certainly no shortage of scholarly works devoted to Nietzsche. My hope is that the present work distinguishes itself from those efforts in that it attempts to move beyond a merely theoretical orientation in order to take up the everyday practice of psychoanalysis in ways that facilitate an appreciation of what clinical practice actually consists in—and not to determine once and for all what this might mean, but rather to appreciate its essential openness and indeterminacy. Although it presumes a willingness to engage with philosophical ways of thinking, at no point does my argument attempt to coast on the seductive purchase that psychoanalytic theory enjoys in the context of a non-clinical, academic audience. As a practicing psychoanalyst my primary intention is to contact clinicians who face the everyday conundrums that psychoanalysis confronts us with, and to demonstrate what a powerful resource Nietzsche can be in any attempt at thinking through the difficulties—clinical, epistemological, and political—that our discipline encounters everywhere today.

No practicing clinician can fail to acknowledge the state of crisis in which the psychoanalytic clinic currently finds itself. With the rise of behavioral, cognitive, and pharmaceutical interventions—supported as they are by a therapeutic marketplace that has become thoroughly industrialized and that is now governed by the demands of economic productivity—psychoanalysis no longer enjoys the esteem it once did. Formerly at the forefront of efforts at outlining a science of psychological experience, psychoanalysis is now largely condemned as a delusional body of knowledge without evidential support. Attempts to respond to such condemnations on their own terms by conducting sound empirical research into the efficacy of analytic treatment routinely fall on deaf ears. Despite the impressive body of empirical literature demonstrating the benefits of an analytic approach, the epithets "evidence-based treatment" and "results-oriented treatment" are used to discredit the psychodynamic field—which functions negatively as their rhetorical opposite—in an international advertising campaign that masquerades as science. What is at stake in this campaign is neither evidence nor science, but an imperative paradigm for determining how the relationship between the individual and the social is to be figured today. The climate of contemporary culture is one in which psychoanalytic thinking seemingly finds no place, and in which a four or five times per week effort at simply saying whatever comes to mind can only appear as an absurd waste of our increasingly, desperately finite financial and temporal resources.

Nietzsche suggests himself as a potential ally of the psychoanalytic clinic to the extent that he diagnosed a similar fate with regard to philosophy over a century ago. For Nietzsche, what passed for philosophy in the context of the nineteenth century German university system was a shameful betrayal of the spirit of genuine philosophical discourse, a rarefied effort at scholarly conformity designed to secure a place for those who were willing to speak in the name of philosophy in exchange for a meager living and a transient, empty reverence. Nietzsche believed himself to be working at a moment in history when Western philosophy was not only in decline but had actually exhausted itself. The few professional academic contemporaries who were aware of his work could not have anticipated the tremendous impact it would subsequently have on European intellectual culture. Those who did appreciate its import, and who were capable for that very reason of appreciating the tragedy of Nietzsche's short, tortured life, could never have anticipated the monstrous appropriations that Nietzsche would suffer at the hands of twentieth century European politics. In every way, Nietzsche lived up to his insistent portrayal of himself as "untimely." My underlying contention is that psychoanalysis today would do well to learn what Nietzsche meant by this.

That being said, and before I am accused of romanticism, the obvious must be stated: An encounter between Nietzsche and psychoanalysis is certainly nothing new. Wherever philosophy has approached psychoanalysis as an object of its claims to an all-encompassing knowledge, references to Nietzsche have always followed in its wake. However, the predominant tendency of efforts to stage such an encounter has been to cast the relationship between Nietzsche and psychoanalysis in terms of Nietzsche's proximity to Freud. More generally, when thinking about the relationship between psychoanalysis and philosophy, "Freud" tends to function metonymically for the broader field of psychoanalysis itself. I hope to show how the relationship between philosophy and psychoanalysis can be expanded in ways that are both clinically specific and post-Freudian in orientation. The more pressing wager of the book is that, by introducing Nietzsche's project into contemporary debates about the nature and function of the psychoanalytic clinic, the future of that clinic can be better secured against efforts to discredit its claims to therapeutic efficacy and to scientific legitimacy. What follows is not a scholarly appreciation of Nietzsche's anticipation of key Freudian themes, but an attempt to demonstrate how what Nietzsche actively practiced in the name of philosophy can help to reinvigorate what psychoanalysis has to offer as an orientation of contemporary clinical practice.

* * *

In Chapter One, I outline basic concepts that guide Nietzsche's thinking and that I believe can be decisive for grasping what is unique to psychoanalysis as a form of treatment: perspectivism, metaphysics, causality, genealogy, *ressentiment*, and will to power. This list is not meant to be exhaustive. Further crucial concepts (bad conscience, nihilism, play) will be elaborated in later chapters; others (eternal return, ascetic ideal, the dice throw, etc.) will necessarily fall outside the purview of this short study, but these should be considered no less clinically illuminating. Throughout, as in each subsequent chapter, I offer clinical vignettes to demonstrate the relevance of Nietzsche's thinking to the everyday events that transpire in the consulting room. This is a long introductory chapter designed to introduce Nietzsche to a clinical audience without prior philosophical experience, in order to pave the way for a more practical appreciation of what Nietzsche has to offer outside the context of the academy.

Chapter Two develops the efforts of the first chapter to integrate what is relevant in Nietzsche's thinking with regard to contemporary clinical practice. Nietzsche's analyses of the ills of modernity are demonstrated to be resonant above all with Helene Deutsch's concept of the "as-if personality" and with the literature that has taken up this concept. Other authors who echo Nietzsche's analyses in this regard include Bion, Ruth Riesenberg Malcolm, Joyce McDougall, and Alan Bass. What is generally at stake is the question of the relationship between what psychoanalysis practices as "interpretation" and what "knowledge" means from a psychoanalytic perspective. I argue that the relationship between knowledge and interpretation in psychoanalysis reflects a relation to knowledge that Nietzsche described as "perspectivism," as against the positivist orientation of contemporary technological science.

Chapter Three focuses on the work of Melanie Klein, with particular attention devoted to the concept of projective identification as this has been taken up as central to contemporary Kleinian and post-Kleinian thought. Where previous efforts to think psychoanalysis and Nietzsche together have traditionally focused on questions about the body and about the neurotic grounds of religious morality, my effort here is to demonstrate how Klein's thinking about the centrality of aggression, splitting, and envy in primitive mental experience brings the insights of psychoanalysis closer to those of Nietzsche than Freudian thought ever did. Reading Nietzsche alongside a selection of key Kleinian texts allows us to appreciate the extent to which Nietzsche anticipated not only those concepts that are central to the classical Freudian tradition (i.e., repression, the id, the super-ego, etc.), but post-Freudian insights into the pre-verbal realm of the pre-oedipal and how to speak to this primarily affective, primitively relational domain.

Chapter Four extends the investigation into this pre-subjective domain essential to post-Freudian psychoanalysis by taking up the concept of "playing" as this is crucial both to Nietzsche and to Donald Winnicott. Nietzsche rehabilitates the concept of "play" at the heart of the pre-Socratic philosopher Heraclitus, in the context of—and as a way of overturning—modern Kantian philosophy. For Nietzsche, play reflects a category of experience that escapes and that cannot be mastered by philosophical discourse. Winnicott similarly presents play as something "that has not yet found a place in the psychoanalytic literature" (1971, p. 41)—a claim that I find still pertinent today. Nietzsche's approach to play allows us to appreciate just how conceptually inventive Winnicott's approach to psychoanalysis is, both at the level of theory and of clinical practice. For Nietzsche and Winnicott, "play" functions both as an object of traditional conceptual reflection, and as a style of discourse that exceeds reflective, conceptual thinking where this is reductively oriented towards factual, conscious understanding. Where the previous chapter argues that Klein brings psychoanalytic thinking closer to Nietzsche than any previous effort, this chapter demonstrates that certain aspects of Winnicott's work unexpectedly bring us close to what might be considered a Nietzschean clinical practice.

Chapter Five engages and compares Nietzsche's philosophical practice with the clinical approach of Jacques Lacan and contemporary Lacanian thought. While the early decades of Lacan's teaching demonstrably belong to the organization of Western philosophy that Nietzsche insistently denounced as "metaphysics," in the final phase of his career Lacan appears to have grasped the orientation of Nietzsche's critique and to have attempted to push psychoanalysis in the direction of what Nietzsche argues for as a non-metaphysical conception of science. With the later Lacan, psychoanalysis accedes to an understanding of itself beyond the classical opposition of theory and practice by abandoning conscious understanding as a viable category for thinking the transformative potential of therapeutic action. Nietzsche had consistently and from the beginning of his project advocated an approach to philosophy beyond the value that traditional moral programs assign to conscious self-reflection. Lacan had similarly, from the outset of his teaching, attempted to divorce the clinical relationship from efforts at applying pre-programmed, standardized procedures. This was to eliminate domination and suggestion from psychoanalysis in order to demonstrate how science might orient itself towards openness and freedom rather than further elaborating closed systems of power and control. Psychoanalysis is a science, for Lacan, to the extent that it refuses to find its basis in identification, suggestion, and control. It took Lacan, like Freud, a lifetime to articulate what this might mean and how this might work, and it was only at the end of his career that Lacan, again like Freud, arrived at a way of thinking that reflects what such a practice might consist in. Serious students of Lacan will undoubtedly accuse me of being too schematic and reductive in distributing his work between early and later phases, as if there were not a tremendous amount of work to be done on what occurred in between. Let me be the first to acknowledge the truth of this accusation. Nevertheless, I hope that those immersed in Lacan and those coming to Lacan for the first time will find much to learn about the Lacanian approach from a comparison with Nietzsche, who is not a typical interlocutor where Lacanian thought is concerned.

* * *

In case it seems that my attempt to put Nietzsche into dialogue with so much in the history of psychoanalysis appears too ambitious, let me reassure the reader that this is not to suggest that Nietzsche had already anticipated *everything* that psychoanalysis has to offer. It is to suggest rather that engaging rigorously with Nietzsche's project can provide a way of organizing what is all too fragmentary in the professional field but that speaks to a desire to affirm psychoanalysis today beyond the confines of what Nietzsche had called "metaphysics." It is only of arid scholarly interest to point out where Nietzsche seems to have come up with some psychoanalytic idea "first." What is more genuinely interesting is the extent to which Nietzsche offers us the possibility of an economy (which is something other than a system) of such ideas, by demonstrating that, whatever their origins in the various psychoanalytic "schools" and despite their differences, they belong to a common discourse at the bottom of which lies a concern with affirming the reality of unconscious processes. Today it seems that those branches of psychoanalysis eager to align themselves with cognitivism and with the neurosciences have largely abandoned any such concern. Those who blindly oppose psychoanalysis in principle share in common this denial of reality, and they, most of all, enjoy an unrestricted freedom in the economic marketplace that drives scientific research forward by deciding, first and foremost and well in advance, what is allowed to describe itself as science and what is not. My experience has left me convinced that the task of psychoanalysis in the twenty-first century is no longer to decipher symbolic meaning, but to cultivate it once again as a real possibility for those who suffer its devastating absence in a world violently bent on realizing spectacular forms of self-destruction. If, as a result, I am occasionally given to imitating Nietzsche by indulging in a somewhat polemical style, hopefully the reader can stay with me long enough to discover the fact that there is nothing at all unscientific about this.

CHAPTER ONE

Nietzsche's perspectivism

The exclusiveness with which the total world-view of modern man, in the second half of the nineteenth century, let itself be determined by the positive sciences and be blinded by the "prosperity" they produced, meant an indifferent turning-away from the questions which are decisive for a genuine humanity. Merely fact-minded sciences make merely fact-minded people.

—Edmund Husserl, *The Crisis of the European Sciences*

E laborating on a series of Nietzsche's ideas drawn from the spectrum of his texts will allow us to judge the extent to which an encounter with Nietzsche can help us in the effort to renew the psychoanalytic clinic. Taking as my point of departure Nietzsche's concept of "perspectivism," I will counter popular readings of Nietzsche still prevalent among analysts who remain interested in the Humanities, in order to provide an outline for a deeper appreciation of Nietzsche's potentially powerful contributions to contemporary clinical practice. My contention is that Nietzsche is to be approached as even more relevant to contemporary psychoanalysis than to the psychoanalysis developed in Freud's day, given the kinds of psychopathology Freud encountered in

Victorian Vienna, and in relation to which psychoanalysis was invented as a theory of the unconscious and as a practice of interpretation—a practice focused more on interpretive *content* than on the nature of the interpretive *process*. Nietzsche allows us to reconsider the practice of interpretation as a technical procedure, and the conditions under which it is effective in facilitating difference, transformation, and change. What follows is an effort at developing Nietzsche's insights into predominant forms of psychopathology that indicates why—despite all insistence to the contrary on the part of the "mental health industry" today—an interpretive, psychodynamic approach remains essential.

Perspectivism and interpretation

Among the claims frequently attributed to Nietzsche these days is the claim, "There are no facts, only interpretations." These words are often invoked either to condemn Nietzsche as a forerunner of postmodern relativism, or to celebrate him as an unexpected friend of liberal democracy. Nietzsche's "perspectivism"—a term that has come to encapsulate his position with regard to an alleged absence of facticity—is regarded either as a defense of the irreducibly subjective character of all human experience, or as a rejection of the enterprise of modern science. Both of these approaches support a long tradition of regarding Nietzsche—whether positively or negatively—as a philosopher who openly celebrated nihilism as a means of embracing the inescapably tragic nature of human life.

Not only are these understandings erroneous, they are not rooted in a faithful reading of Nietzsche's texts. In fact, Nietzsche never wrote, "There are no facts, only interpretations." Distorted and taken out of context—a gesture which, again, has a long history in the reception of Nietzsche's work—these words refer to a passage in *Book Three* of the series of fragments posthumously assembled as his *magnum opus* by his notoriously inept sister, to which she gave the title *The Will to Power*—the title of a book Nietzsche himself intended but never actually managed to write. Here is the passage in full:

> Against positivism, which halts at phenomena—"There are *only facts*"—I would say: No, facts is precisely what there is not, only interpretations. We cannot establish any fact "in itself": Perhaps it is folly to want to do such a thing.

"Everything is subjective," you say; but even this is interpretation. The "subject" is not something given, it is something added and invented and projected behind what there is. —Finally, is it necessary to posit an interpreter behind the interpretation? Even this is invention, hypothesis.

In so far as the word "knowledge" has any meaning, the world is knowable; but it is *interpretable* otherwise, it has no meaning behind it, but countless meanings. —"Perspectivism."

It is our needs that interpret the world; our drives and their For and Against. Every drive is a kind of lust to rule; each one has its perspective that it would like to compel all the other drives to accept as a norm. (1968a, p. 267)

At first it might seem that one does no injustice to Nietzsche's thinking by reducing the first paragraph of the passage to the statement, "There are no facts, only interpretations." After all, was not Nietzsche a master of the aphoristic style, and are we not simply helping him along by cleaning up what were mere notes that could just as well have been put forth as a bold, concise statement of his philosophy? Hardly. The actual statement and the form in which it is popularly inherited today could not be more dissimilar. The first sentence of the second paragraph of this short passage—"'Everything is subjective,' you say; but even this is interpretation"—should be enough to indicate that Nietzsche had already anticipated what has become the common misunderstanding of his position. To say that there are "*only* interpretations" is not to say that there are "*merely* interpretations," as if facts were beyond the reach of the human mind, bound as it is to its own particular, subjective position. Furthermore, the notion of a "subjective position" in the sense of a limited regard with respect to the objective truth of a given phenomenon, is not at all what Nietzsche intends with the word "perspective." To imagine that Nietzsche's views on the perspectival character of experience indicates his belief that no access to "things-in-themselves" is objectively possible is to confuse Nietzsche with Kant, whom he openly ridiculed. When Nietzsche writes, in response to the anticipated charge of subjectivism, "but even this is interpretation," he is telling us that we have misunderstood what is at stake in the claim that "facts [are] *precisely* what there is not, only interpretations." For Nietzsche, facts are not opposed to interpretations in the way that objectivity is opposed to subjectivity, things-in-themselves opposed to mere appearances. Facts are species of interpretation that express inhibition or "weakness."

By "positivism" Nietzsche means a way of organizing a scientific attitude by reducing conditions of subjectivity in favor of increasing conditions of objectivity. This is not necessarily the same as (though it is not unrelated to) positivism as a particular, historical, philosophical school. Nietzsche's understanding of positivism indicates the way in which objectivity is equated with what is "good," while subjectivity is equated with what is "bad"—hence the effort to accede to the one at the expense of the other. Nietzsche thus grasps that positivism is a moral attitude that insists on the inherent goodness of universal, objective truths. The basis for this moral evaluation is the democratic community: What is objective brings us together in that it can be universally shared, whereas what is subjective rends us apart and thereby encourages power and domination. Nietzsche traces this way of thinking back to Socrates and Plato, demonstrating how it has evolved through institutional Christianity into modern technological science. As against this positivist attitude—positive in a dual sense, in that it claims to deal with "facts" that are assumed to be by definition "good"—Nietzsche's perspectivism names a way of thinking that grasps how that which presents itself as rigorously and eternally logical does not necessarily coincide with efforts to enhance life. Perspectivism challenges the positivist version of science that opposes the objective and the subjective, facts and interpretations, and that does so by constructing and evaluating these oppositions according to a moral logic of right and wrong.

Babette Babich (1994) makes clear that what is at issue in the passage at hand is Nietzsche's critique of the claims to knowledge of modern science (pp. 37–42). The reference to scientific positivism, she contends, is indissociable from Nietzsche's claim concerning the relationship between facts and interpretation. Far from making a general claim about perspectival singularity as barring access to objective truth, Nietzsche is attempting to demonstrate that the claim of modern science to objective truth is itself a form of interpretation. Rather than attempting to restrict us from making statements about objectivity, he is actually encouraging our desire to do so, by clarifying what such a gesture actually consists in. It is positivist science itself that "halts"; Nietzsche's insistence is not that it must do so, but that in doing so science fails to become truly scientific. The positivist claim that there are "only facts" is guided by a resentful negativity that Nietzsche's assertion that there are "only interpretations" actively intends to counter and to overturn. Nietzsche is not insisting that there is no truth, but that truth is not what science in its contemporary form interprets it to be.

Babich further argues that Nietzsche here anticipates those who will respond from a logical framework by disqualifying the statement that there are "only interpretations" as self-refuting: If there are no facts, only interpretations, then Nietzsche contradicts himself by offering this not as interpretation but as fact. Nietzsche is not so naive as to not be fully aware of this contradiction and to not be deploying it in an altogether deliberate way: "'Everything is subjective,' you say; but even this is interpretation." This charge can be spoken by the interlocutor, who interprets Nietzsche to mean, "everything is subjective," and then claims that this is only his own subjective position. At the same time, Nietzsche has positioned himself so as to be capable of taking this same stance, but with a different emphasis: To interpret his meaning as "everything is subjective" is itself a failure to grasp what is being asserted by continuing to associate interpretation with subjectivity—as if interpretation were merely the activity of an underlying subject. "The 'subject' is not something given," Nietzsche continues, "it is something added and invented and projected behind what there is." The subject or self is not the one who interprets, but is itself an effect of interpretive processes.

"Finally," the paragraph concludes, "is it necessary to posit an interpreter behind the interpretation? Even this is invention, hypothesis." What the interlocutor who understands Nietzsche as having asserted that "everything is subjective"—that perspectivism indicates a limit on claims to self-understanding rather than an invitation to greater self-invention—fails to appreciate is that interpretation is not to be conceived as the activity of an underlying subject, and that to figure interpretation in this way is itself an interpretation, one guided by a metaphysical project that opposes the subjective and the objective. In the passage from *The Will to Power* that appears just prior to this, Nietzsche writes, "There is no question of 'subject and object,' but of a particular species of animal that can prosper only through a certain relative rightness; above all, regularity of its perceptions (so that it can accumulate experience)" (1968a, p. 266). All talk of subjectivity and objectivity, which defines the general horizon of the secular, scientific worldview, is an effort to establish a framework for regularity, predictability, and calculation in an interpretation of truth as the correspondence between these two terms.

Those who would immediately interpret Nietzsche as having asserted, "everything is subjective," are attempting to figure his insights in familiar terms, reducing their impact and defending against the incursion of new perspectives. It is positivism, and to the extent that this can be traced back to Kant's version of philosophy as an effort at policing what counts as scientifically viable and what does not, that is complicit with postmodern, nihilistic relativism, not Nietzsche.

Knowledge, for Nietzsche, is not reducible to the accumulation of facts, in the same way that interpretations and perspectives are not "subjective" phenomena. To interpret is not to express, "This is how I see things ..."—an interpretation is not the expression of an "I think ...". "In so far as the word 'knowledge' has any meaning," Nietzsche writes, indicating that there absolutely *is* knowledge, fact, but that these are not eternal or immutable, "the world is knowable; but it is *interpretable* otherwise, it has no meaning behind it, but countless meanings. —'Perspectivism.'" Perspectivism is here conceived as a practice of interpretation. The world is knowable not because it has *a* meaning, but countless meanings. To state that the world "has no meaning *behind* it" is not to deny nihilistically the meaningfulness of experience, it is to refuse an interpretation of meaning as singular and universal, lying "behind" the veil of appearance. Unlike positivism, perspectivism is not nihilism in that it does not deny meaning (value) to experience, rather it refuses to split meaning and experience apart in the first place. Interpretation is not the activity of a subject discerning underlying meaning, but the pre-subjective projection of a multiplicity of meanings or possibilities that constitute the world's phenomenal surface. In *The Birth of Tragedy*, Nietzsche had called this creative projection "Dionysian wisdom" (Safranski, 2000/2003).

The fourth and final paragraph should appear the most striking, especially to psychoanalysts. So far Nietzsche has undercut everything that Freud aspired to establish: the psychical reality of the ego; the capacity of interpretation to arrive at truth; the objectivity of claims to scientific knowledge in the study of mind. But here Nietzsche ventures onto territory that psychoanalysis as a discipline specifically claims for itself: "It is our needs that interpret the world; our drives and their For and Against. Every drive is a kind of lust to rule; each one has its perspective that it would like to compel all the other drives to accept as a norm." How are analysts to encounter the notion that it is not the subject who interprets, but the drives themselves? This claim would seem to cut to the core of both a theory of treatment and a theory of mind, yet perhaps it does so in such a way that illuminates what links them together. If, "It is our needs that interpret the world," what is the analyst doing besides reacting to the patient's discourse with her own countertransferential projections? If it is not the analyst's subjectivity that interprets, but the drives themselves that in doing so produce an illusory sense of professional identity, can psychoanalysis be regarded as anything more than a form of suggestion? When Nietzsche describes the practice of interpretation as an event that takes place not at the level of the subject or ego but of the drives themselves, supplementing this with, "Every drive is a kind of lust to rule," no clinician will fail to recognize how deeply unsettling are the moral implications of this claim. Would Nietzsche have sided with those who accuse psychoanalysts of engaging in a power relationship intended to impose their perspectives as to what constitutes reality on their patients? Can interpretation as a therapeutic procedure ever contain any power beyond that of suggestion?

This last question haunted Freud to the end of his career, impelling him continuously to rework his most fundamental ideas. Today this question threatens the future of the Freudian clinic because psychoanalysis has never truly opened itself to the resources needed to think this problem through—resources that are to be found in Nietzsche's writings. A rigorous encounter between psychoanalysis and Nietzschean perspectivism—which is not the same as a scholarly appreciation of the occasional proximities of Nietzsche and Freud—is short-circuited by the anxieties evoked by passages such as the one quoted above. The phrase, "Every drive is a kind of lust to rule" will conjure popular images of Nietzsche as a madman who celebrated the exercise of power in war, militarism, and domination. "Lust to rule" is the common misinterpretation of the title of the work in which these words appear: *The Will to Power*. As several commentators on Nietzsche's work have exhausted themselves in attempting to make clear, "will to power" is not "lust to rule," though it is not unrelated to (at times it even strategically celebrates) this vulgar, metaphysical interpretation. Interpretation, perspective, and will to power in Nietzsche's writings are, while not synonymous, irreducibly linked in a conceptual economy within which there is no possibility of discussing one in the absence of the others. Interpretation is an expression of will to power; will to power creates perspective; perspective, when it affirms itself as such, opens the horizon of further and more complex interpretations. There is nothing of a subject's desire to dominate an object in any of this. As a pre-subjective event rooted in the body rather than in metaphysical conceptions of mind or soul, a drive is constitutively interpretive in its essentially relational determination as both "For and Against." There is no drive outside a multiplicity of drives, no force without another force forcing against it. For Nietzsche, drive is an inherently relational phenomenon. The very drivenness of the drive as individuating-relational process is what Nietzsche calls "will to power," which relentlessly pursues not some object but "perspective, the basic condition of life" (1886/1989a, p. 2).

Metaphysics

In a famous aphorism from *Beyond Good and Evil: A Prelude to a Philosophy of the Future*, Nietzsche (1886/1989a) writes,

> "I have done that," says my memory. "I cannot have done that," says my pride, and remains inexorable. Eventually—memory yields. (p. 80)

With good reason, Walter Kaufman sees in this statement a foreshadowing of Freud's theory of repression (ibid., fn. 3). One could very well conceive of repression as a "yielding" of memory to the "pride" of the ego in its efforts to negotiate the demands of the id, superego, and external world, though Nietzsche's emphasis would appear to be on the narcissistic dimension of the ego rather than on its adaptive qualities. However, as is so often the case in Nietzsche's writings, there are several ways of reading this passage. It is not clear whether Nietzsche is describing an essentially pathological or healthy condition—nor whether these would be in any way be opposed. For Freud, repression is not an inherently pathological process, and it is not repression but the failure of repression—the *return* of the repressed—that leads to symptom formation. Freud, however, does not conceive of repression as a life-enhancing operation, at least not in Nietzsche's sense, only in a reactive sense: in the service of environmental adaptation. Nietzsche consistently disregards any association of adaptation with the promotion of what he calls "life." For Nietzsche, life has to do not with adaptation and survival, but with the pursuit of intensity and affective extremes. Life as will to power does not seek to extend itself indefinitely through bare survival, but to risk itself—even if unsustainably—in the pursuit of the singular and the unique. Is Nietzsche here describing an effort to adapt to reality reactively as it stands or actively to force reality out of joint?

On one reading, Nietzsche might be describing weakness of the will as an inability to encounter and to assimilate difference in order to affirm itself. Splitting itself into a present form incapable of enduring its own past, such a weak will would not be able to appropriate the past as a resource for driving itself forward onto further expressions of power. The "yielding" of memory would thus constitute a reactive "no" that refuses the past. "Pride" would in this sense describe an inhibition, a barrier to accepting the truth about oneself. This is the familiar sense of Freudian repression, which supports an approach to treatment as an effort at "making the unconscious conscious"—uncovering the essential truth about the patient's experience in the form of a meaningful origin that would explain everything about his suffering, and in such a way that would bring that suffering to a close.

On another reading, Nietzsche is describing a positive power of forgetfulness as the ability to be done with the past, to organize memory in such a way that the sting of past defeat does not repeat itself. The "yielding" of memory to pride on this reading means that memory in an ordinary sense precisely does not emerge: The link between memory and consciousness is successfully avoided. This is not to suggest that the past is "erased," but rather that it does not reemerge in ways that interfere with the potential for being open towards a different future through action. Such a mode of forgetfulness would not be defensive but creative, life-enhancing rather than symptom-producing. It is therefore not a question of what the "strong" are capable of doing that the "weak" cannot do, but of the effects that the very same gesture produces where conditions of strength or weakness generally predominate.

For Freud, the return of the repressed results in a defensive compromise expressed symptomatically. For Nietzsche, the return of the repressed results in conscious self-awareness, as the greater symptom of which lesser symptoms are always symptomatic. According to Gilles Deleuze (1962/1983):

> [...] consciousness is defined less in relation to exteriority (in terms of the real) than in relation to superiority (in terms of values). This

distinction is essential to a general conception of consciousness
and the unconscious. In Nietzsche consciousness is always the consciousness of an inferior in relation to a superior to which he is
subordinated or into which he is "incorporated." (p. 39)

This is to say that, just as for Freud, the ego and the quality of consciousness that is attached to it emerge in response to an inhibition of
energetic "discharge" brought on by encounters with forces capable of
subordinating it through displays of greater strength. From a developmental perspective, consciousness would be the symptom of the child's
fundamental helplessness in the face of a world that it initially cannot master. When efforts to manipulate the world by means of fantasy
and hallucination inevitably fail, the result is the elaboration of an
"I think ..." itself no more than an organizationally more sophisticated
and more tenacious form of fantasy. Freud describes something not
unlike this in his paper, "Formulations on the two principles of mental
functioning" (1911b):

> Restraint upon motor discharge (upon action), which then became
> necessary, was provided by means of the process of *thinking*, which
> was developed from the presentation of ideas. Thinking was
> endowed with characteristics which made it possible for the men-
> tal apparatus to tolerate an increased tension of stimulus while the
> process of discharge was postponed. It is essentially an experimen-
> tal kind of acting, accompanied by displacement of relatively small
> quantities of cathexis together with less expenditure (discharge) of
> them. (p. 221; emphasis in original)

"Presentation of ideas" describes the quality of consciousness, initially
a correlate of sensation, becoming itself a source of internal stimuli.
"Thinking" describes the coordination of these stimuli into an ongoing
activity. Freud regards thought as an "experimental form of action"—
an effect of inhibition. The identification of the experience of conscious
awareness and thought is an effect of the inhibition of action: "Small
quantities of cathexis" substitute for the more immediately desirable
experience of active bodily discharge. When the baby cannot effectively act, it thinks. This does not mark a failure of action turning into
"mere" thought, but the way in which the apparently coherent oppositions between thought and action, fantasy and reality, gradually and

NIETZSCHE'S PERSPECTIVISM   11

intrinsically, dynamically and repeatedly dissolve at the unconscious origins of psychic life. For the infant there are no sharp distinctions to be drawn between thought, fantasy, perception, and hallucination. Freud derives a positive account of the development of cognitive faculties from out this scene of original, primary disorganization. Nietzsche insistently emphasizes the interference of consciousness as a reactive, inhibited form of what would otherwise emerge as integrated psychical-bodily activity.

As Deleuze makes clear in the passage just cited, for Nietzsche consciousness does not emerge as an effort to adapt to the demands of reality, but as a means of revenging oneself upon those very demands. Thinking does not reflect adaptation to reality but revenge against existence as fundamental injustice. This is the primitive developmental origin of all moral sensibility. Reality is experienced as constitutively "unfair"; moral sentiment is an elaborate condemnation of the contingency of the real. The development of consciousness into an ongoing faculty that defines an experience of self as enduring substance or as uncircumventible ground is rooted in a hatred of reality as that which constantly and relentlessly imposes environmental demand on the dynamic organization and expression of the drives. Meaning-making becomes an effort at creating a moral case against the perceived injustice of the influx of chance and difference. As for Freud, conscious thought is an effect of subordinated action. Nietzsche perceives the way in which this subordination develops itself according to the "spirit of revenge." The spirit of revenge describes a relation to reality where obsessive, conscious reflection substitutes for spontaneous, creative activity.

According to Nietzsche, the spirit of revenge is derivative of the will's incapacity to reverse the order of time and to undo painful situations that it has suffered. Instead of evoking laughter, the spirit of revenge intends to erase the past, which is to say that life turns against itself: "Memory yields." Revenge stems from the irreversibility of time, which makes the will incapable of freeing itself from the burden of the past:

> "It was": That is what the will's teeth-gnashing and most lonely affliction is called. Powerless against that which has been done, the will is an angry spectator of all things past.
> The will cannot will backwards; that it cannot break time and time's desire—that is the will's most lonely affliction. (1884/1961, p. 161)

The inability of finite being to undo the past does not mean that the will stops trying to do so. To the contrary, the quixotic attempt to reverse the order of time is precisely what the spirit of revenge consists in: "[…] this alone is *revenge* itself: the will's antipathy towards time and time's 'It was'" (p. 162). Trying to eliminate the past cause of the present effects from which it suffers, the will becomes not only aware of, but consumed with, the order of causality. Gianni Vattimo (2000/2006) writes, "From this experience is born the vision of Being as a structure of cause and effect, of the foundational and the founded: The principle of causality that dominates our representation of the world is an expression of the instinct of revenge, the most profound instinct of all" (p. 16). The fantasy of redemption from the irreversibility of time lies at the heart of all metaphysical thinking; it gathers together and demonstrates the complicity of basic conceptual oppositions that it would otherwise seem unusual to compare or to challenge.

The ordinary way of portraying Nietzsche's account of metaphysics is in terms of the positing of an extratemporal, ideal world beyond the everyday flux of matter and time—a privileging of Being over becoming. But this is the result of metaphysical thinking, not its founding gesture. In *Twilight of the Idols* (1888/1968b) Nietzsche defines metaphysics in terms of "four great errors":

1. the error of confusing cause and effect;
2. the error of false causation;
3. the error of imaginary causes;
4. the error of free will.

Metaphysics constitutes a framework that supports itself by linking together profound misunderstandings of the nature of causality, freedom, and the will. Reversing the order of cause and effect, devising false and imaginary causes, attributing the power of causation to the alleged free will of an agent (whether human or divine) all contribute to an interpretation of life as unjustifiable suffering. By confusing or reversing cause and effect, suffering from the burden of the past is alleviated through efforts at meaning-making. By insisting on false causal connections between unrelated events, experience appears more deeply meaningful than it actually is. By attributing imaginary causes (i.e., "God's will") to the origin of these false connections, grandiose explanatory frameworks evolve that seem capable of accounting for the origin of experience as such. One such pervasive mythical explanation is the alleged freedom of the subject to willingly choose whatever happens in the course of "its" life:

> We have always believed we know what a cause is: But whence did we derive our knowledge, more precisely our belief we possessed this knowledge? From the realm of the celebrated "inner facts", none of which has up till now been shown to be factual. We believed ourselves to be causal agents in the act of willing; we at least thought we were there *catching causality in the act*. It was likewise never doubted that all the *antecedentia* of an action, its causes, were to be sought in consciousness and could be discovered there if we sought them—as "motives": for otherwise one could not have been *free* to perform it, *responsible* for it. Finally, who would have disputed that a thought is caused? that the ego causes the thought? [...] Of these three "inner facts" through which causality seemed to be guaranteed the first and most convincing was that of *will as cause*; the conception of a consciousness ("mind") as cause and later still that of the ego (the "subject") as cause are merely after-products, after causality had, on the basis of will, been firmly established as a given fact, as *empiricism* [...] Meanwhile, we have thought better. Today we do not believe a word of it. The "inner world" is full of phantoms and false lights: the will is one of them. (1888/1968b, p. 60)

As a phantom of the inner world—itself a phantom—the will is not the possession of a subject or ego, but what drives an experience of self *as* self to express itself (or not) as a striving toward individuation. Metaphysics is a compulsive seeking after origins, first causes from which meaning ultimately issues and in terms of which experience can be made to account for itself. This arises when one begins to suffer the irreversibility of time and the burden of past experiences and to treat these in the spirit of revenge. The pursuit of knowledge—figured as a moral project, in which "truth" is approached as inherently "good"—becomes a way of repudiating experience as an encounter with chance, unpredictability, and the unknown.

Clinical example

B works in a highly competitive, corporate environment that she complains causes her an unbearable amount of distress for which she sought therapeutic help. She feels chronically subordinated by her supervisors and worries that she might at any moment lose her job due to no fault of her own. One day she arrives at her analysis and relates the following scene. At her office, she had gotten up from her desk and walked down the hallway toward the bathroom. Just as she was doing so, a coworker rushed past her in tears and made it into the bathroom before her. Without wondering what this was all about, B proceeded into the bathroom and though she felt a great deal of empathy for the woman sobbing in the stall next to her, she respectfully did not say a word. When B emerged from the bathroom, she encountered her supervisor hovering just outside the door. The supervisor began to berate her for attempting to comfort her coworker, who had just been fired for reasons that did not concern B, threatening that she had better not interfere with administrative procedures if she did not want to meet a similar fate. B stood stunned, silent, internalizing all of this, and then casually walked back to her desk as if nothing had happened, not just concealing but at first not even realizing the fact that, as became clear when our session drew near, she had been shaken to her core.

In the session with me B was able to express all of the terrible anxiety that she had bottled up since the event. She pleaded with me, as if addressing the supervisor she dared not cross: "What was going on? All I was doing was going to the bathroom! I had no idea that this woman had just been fired! My supervisor was acting like I was being insubordinate. She probably felt bad about what she had done and was just taking it out on me. I know she's not really the bitch she has to act like in front of us or else she's the one who would lose her job. So why does she have to act that way towards me? What did I do wrong? Can you explain this to me?"

What struck me in B's demand that I explain to her the actions of her supervisor was the fact that, given everything she had previously told me about this woman and the general atmosphere of her work environment, it seemed to me that she had already explained the supervisor's outburst perfectly well. B had had nothing to do with the situation, but by chance had found herself on the receiving end of the supervisor's aggression. No doubt this had been unpleasant and I had no reason to disagree with her explanation. But then why was she not satisfied with the explanation she herself had already given? Why was she asking me to tell her about the meaning of her experience when she had already accurately perceived that it had had nothing whatsoever to do with her?

Such an ordinary clinical moment illustrates the relevance of what Nietzsche meant by as grand and as intimidating a term as "metaphysics." B might just as well have laughed at the absurdity of her supervisor's behavior and forgotten about the incident altogether. Instead, it weighed upon her heavily, as if it were a symbolic condensation of all the difficulties she faced in her life. What was traumatic in the scenario she described was not just the supervisor's aggressiveness, but its inexplicable, meaningless connection to her own actions. Although she could explain perfectly well the psychological motivations behind the supervisor's irrational behavior, what she could not explain—what could not be explained—was *why this had happened to her*. There is no answer to this question, but in the context of metaphysical thinking an explanation appears to be the only way to reduce anxiety.

Clinically speaking, we can understand metaphysics as what programs the question, "What did I do to deserve this?" as if there were some cosmic meaning behind the injustices that people suffer in their everyday lives. Of course, often there is an explanation, but there is certainly nothing metaphysical about it: In her analysis B endlessly prompts me for coping strategies to help her deal with the anxieties that working in such an uncaring, corporate environment provokes in her. Nietzsche would see in this the error of reversing cause and effect: The real question B will one day have to face is not, "what am I doing to deserve this?" but, "why am I subjecting myself to these insufferable conditions in the first place?" Reversing the order of cause and effect, metaphysics insistently seeks after meaning where there is none to be found, in order to relieve primitive anxieties evoked by meaninglessness, inexplicability, and chance.

Interpretation, explanation, genealogy

In a notebook entry dated between June and July of 1885, Nietzsche (2003) writes:

> In the realm of the inorganic, too, for an atom of force only its direct proximity counts: Forces at a distance cancel one another out. Here we find the core of perspectivism, and the reason why a living being is "egoistic" through and through. (p. 25)

Nietzsche often dismisses efforts to distinguish absolutely between the organic and the inorganic, which is to say between "life" and its "opposite." For Nietzsche, there is no other of life, nothing that would guarantee or justify the claim to existence of what is alive and can declare itself as such through its actions; it is from a failure to appreciate this that a fictional, eternal other of life provided by claims to moral order derives. Morality is the sign of a failure to think the organic and the inorganic together, to acknowledge the ways in which the inorganic can be made to act upon and to shape the organic, and in such a way that proves the reality of "action at a distance" (the effects that Socrates and Christ, for instance, continue to produce to this day as a result of the power of the written word). To say that "forces at a distance cancel one another out" is not to deny but rather to affirm this principle, the reality of which Nietzsche had asserted in a notebook entry of the same period: "[…] it is the will to power which guides the inorganic world as well, or rather, that there *is* no inorganic world. 'Action at a distance' cannot be eliminated: *something draws something else closer, something feels drawn*" (p. 15).

Why is this "the core of perspectivism," and why is it "the reason why a living being is 'egoistic' through and through"? In a longer note that immediately follows the one quoted above Nietzsche writes:

> The weaker pushes its way to the stronger, out of a lack of food; it wants to take shelter, if possible to become *one* with it. Conversely, the stronger repulses the weaker, it doesn't want to perish in this way; instead, as it grows it splits into two and more. The greater the urge to unity, the more one may infer weakness; the more there is an urge to variety, differentiation, inner fragmentation, the more force is present.
>
> The drive to come closer and the drive to repulse something—in both the inorganic and the organic world, these are what binds. The whole distinction is a prejudice.
>
> The will to power in every combination of forces—*resisting what's stronger, attacking what's weaker*—is more correct. *Processes as "beings"*. (p. 25)

Nietzsche here is using the term "egoistic" to denote this tendency of strength to refuse unity, to differentiate itself against the pull of the weak toward mere adaptation and bare survival. The presence of greater force expresses itself as "inner fragmentation"—a term that no psychoanalyst would think to associate with the strength of the ego.

What allows Nietzsche to do so is the fact that he does not treat the ego as an adaptive agency, but as an ecstatic, perspectival multiplicity. This is why he conceives living beings as "egoistic" *qua* will to power. The "core of perspectivism" is the understanding of life as will to power—as irreducibly multiple conflict of forces—of force *as* relation—of the combination of forces that "binds." "Inner fragmentation" is not the falling apart of a previously integrated unity, but the active differentiation of what binds forces together relationally ("*Processes as 'beings'*").

With the term "perspective" then, Nietzsche intends to draw a sharp distinction between interpretation and explanation: Interpretation creates perspectives. Explanation establishes positive facts. The latter are mere inhibited versions of the former. An explanation is an interpretation that fails to register its essential openness to further interpretation, returning what is different into what is familiar:

> Properties are not explained by the history of their genesis. They must already be known. *Historical* explanation is the reduction to a sequence we are *used to*: by means of analogy. (p. 5)

> What is "knowing"? Tracing something alien back to something one is acquainted and familiar with. First principle: What we have *got used to* we no longer consider a riddle, a problem. The feeling of the new, of the discomfiting, is dulled: Everything that happens *regularly* no longer seems questionable to us. This is why the knower's first instinct is to *look for the rule* ... Hence the superstition of the physicists: Where they can stand still, i.e., where the regularity of phenomena allows them to apply abbreviating formulas, they think *knowing* has taken place. They have a feeling of "security", but behind this intellectual security is the soothing of their fearfulness: *They want the rule* because it strips the world of dreadfulness. *Fear of the unpredictable* as the *hidden instinct* of science. (p. 107)

> What alone can *knowing* be? "Interpretation", *not* "explanation". (p. 76)

An explanation reflects a closed system of reading, a determination of phenomena in terms of facts that do not permit further elaboration. This is the sense in which science, in its present form, "halts at phenomena." Interpretation, on the other hand, is not so inhibited. For Nietzsche, an interpretive practice recognizes no rule and does not seek after knowledge in a classical sense (as universal or objective). The "knowledge" produced by interpretation is radically singular—*perspectival*. Perspectival knowledge is not universally shared but the product of local organizations and hierarchies of force capable of shaping other such organizations—of "commanding."

Perspective is thus not the perspective *of* consciousness. Interpretation, for Nietzsche, does not "expand" consciousness toward the adoption of ever greater or more encompassing perspectives (p. 10). Perspective reflects rather the hierarchical ordering of forces (drives). It is not the most dominant drive that produces an effect of consciousness, but the lowest, most subordinated drives that produce consciousness to the extent that they are inhibited from expression through action. Perspective is the origin of this consciousness-effect; it is an ordering or rank that produces an effect of consciousness that takes itself as origin or as truth. It may be the case that such a hierarchical organization of drives holds sway for long periods of time, but their reorganization is inevitable given the primary, "Dionysian" character of the world as becoming or as will to power:

> Fundamental question: Whether the *perspectival* is part of the *essence*, and not just a form of regarding, a relation between various beings? Do the various forces stand in relation to one another, in such a way that this relation is tied to the viewpoint of perception? This would be possible *if everything that is were essentially something that perceives*. (p. 107)

To say "the *perspectival* is part of the *essence*" is to challenge the classical notion of "essence" as immutable, atemporal "Being." To say that perspective is "not just a form of regarding"—again, not just a subjective "angle" or "point of view" from which consciousness perceives something—that it is not just "a relation between various beings"— beings whose essence would preexist or stand outside the flux of becoming—is to say that there is no Being, no atemporal immutability. When Nietzsche asks whether the relation that obtains between forces is related to perception, he is asking whether this relation is open to further redistribution, to the production of new perspectives. To say that, "This would be possible *if everything that is were essentially something that perceives*," is to affirm this openness, as another way of asserting that there is no singular Being, no substance, that all existence is the confluence of dynamically open systems of relationality or becoming—no objects, no subjects, only relational engagements of force that continuously act on and modify one another:

> The triumphant concept of "force", with which our physicists have created God and the world, needs supplementing: It must be ascribed an inner world which I call "will to power", i.e., an insatiable craving to manifest power; or to employ, exercise power, as a creative drive, etc. (p. 26)

What does it mean to ascribe to the notion of force or drive an "inner world," and to identify this with "will to power"? Force is not the possession of a given body, it is not an effect but the cause of a body as a complex of relations of force in the absence of any absolute distinction between inside and outside, self and world, organic and inorganic. Drives do not belong to a body; a body and its actions are the product of a given state of forces or drives. This is a correlate of the absence of any stable, atemporal Being:

> "Timeless" to be rejected. At a particular moment of force, an absolute conditionality of the redistribution of all its forces is given: It cannot stand still. 'Change' is part of the essence, and therefore so is temporality—which, however, amounts to just one more conceptual positing of the necessity of change. (p. 21)

As the essence of the drive, the "inner world" of force—will to power—*is* change, which is another word here for becoming. Nietzsche links this essence to time: "temporality." Temporality, however, as the linear progression from past to present to future, is merely an intellectually abstract "conceptual positing" of change as "necessity"—it is an abstract rendition of change or becoming in terms of distinct beings (i.e., past, present, and future). Will to power names a different conception of time: Time as the irreducibility of change or of becoming without essence, which is to say without the hypostatized forms of past, present, and future. The necessity of change is the essence of becoming, which is to say that this essence is determined otherwise than as an atemporal or eternal "now"—it is not *the* essence in the form of a hidden underlying thing, but the essentially changing nature of change—an "inner world" that would constitute the drivenness of the drive, the forcefulness of force, which is to say force as inherently multiple and self-differentiating. This is what Nietzsche calls "will to power" as agonistic, individuating-relational ("egoistic") process.

The impulse to metaphysics expresses an effort to reduce this complexity in favor of causal explanations that identify simple, underlying essences. This is implicitly an effort to refuse difference, novelty, and time—in Nietzsche's terms: to insist on the priority of Being over becoming. The opposite effort—to figure Being *as* becoming—is what Nietzsche calls "genealogy." As a classically trained philologist, Nietzsche understood and deployed this term not in its everyday metaphysical sense—as a tracing back to historical origins—but as an attempt to account for the contingencies of development and to demonstrate that what lies at the origin of any given state of affairs is not some singular, enveloping ground, but complex lines of intersection between chance and necessity. Metaphysics always intends to discover unity in the past, in such a way that provides causal explanation; genealogy discovers hierarchy and difference—chance. Another way to state this would be to say that for a genealogical approach, the question of a thing's essence is the question of its meaning and value, not its objective truth.

Metaphysics always returns us to singular, causal origins; genealogy uncovers the precariousness of experience and demonstrates how things could easily have been completely otherwise. In the chapter from *Twilight of the Idols* (1888/1968b) discussed above, Nietzsche diagnoses the "psychological motivation" for the "four great errors":

> To trace something unknown back to something known is alleviating, soothing, gratifying and gives moreover a feeling of power. Danger, disquiet, anxiety attend the unknown—the first instinct is to *eliminate* these distressing states. First principle: Any explanation is better than none. Because it is at bottom only a question of wanting to get rid of oppressive ideas, one is not exactly particular about what means one uses to get rid of them: The first idea which explains that the unknown is in fact the known does so much good that one "holds it for true". Proof by *pleasure* ("by potency") as criterion of truth. —The cause-creating drive is thus conditioned and excited by the feeling of fear. The question "why?" should furnish, if at all possible, not so much the cause for its own sake as a *certain kind of cause*—a soothing, liberating, alleviating cause. That

something already *known*, experienced, inscribed in the memory is posited as cause is the first consequence of this need. The new, the unexperienced, the strange is excluded from being cause. (p. 62)

In the psychoanalytic literature, similar statements abound concerning not just the defensive efforts on the part of patients who compulsively substitute the known for the unknown, but on the part of analysts themselves when theory fails to reflect the nuances of clinical experience. To cite but a few relevant examples from a vast array of important contributions: Winnicott (1971) and Bion (1962/1984a) need no introduction in this regard; Ogden (1989) describes an "unconscious fear of not knowing," which is defended against through the deployment of substitute formations that "create for the individual the illusion of knowing and of being" (p. 8); Rose (2000) posits an "anxiety of change" in the face of unpredictability and the chance that reality is not always what it immediately appears to be; Casement's admirable *Learning from the Patient* (1985) is centered around this very theme:

> By listening too readily to accepted theories, and to what they lead the practitioner to expect, it is easy to become deaf to the unexpected. When a therapist thinks that he can see signs of what is familiar to him, he can become blind to what is different and strange [...] the unknown is treated as if it were already known. (p. 9)

As the chapters that follow will attempt to make increasingly clear, Nietzsche's refusal to consider the experience of knowledge as inherently beneficial, but rather as dysfunctionally self-protective—a position thoroughly at odds with classical theories of therapeutic action—finds ample echoes in the contemporary clinical literature. Nietzsche provides an opportunity for coordinating these crucial, non-classical insights from across the spectrum of psychoanalytic perspectives.

Ressentiment

The spirit of revenge that animates all metaphysical thinking is otherwise conceived by Nietzsche in affective terms as *"ressentiment."* This is among the most central of Nietzsche's concepts, and its development is perhaps his most important contribution to psychology. Although it might be translated as "resentment," Nietzsche's decision to leave the French term untranslated is designed to emphasize its essentially aggressive, destructive character (in Chapter three I argue that Melanie Klein rediscovered and expanded on this concept when she put envy at the center of psychic development). *Ressentiment* reflects life turning against itself by refusing difference and variation, substituting for these logics of opposition and sameness, ruining efforts at individuation and hierarchy. Although when it becomes conscious it is felt as pain, unconsciously *ressentiment* is a source of immense satisfaction.

Deleuze (1962/1983) put the concepts of *active* and *reactive* force at the forefront of his approach to Nietzsche's thinking. Rejecting in particular Heidegger's (1961/1991a, 1961/1991b) efforts to demonstrate a systematic underpinning to Nietzsche's thought (elaborated around the primary axes of will to power and eternal return), Deleuze provided a reading of Nietzsche that would prove decisive not just for Nietzsche studies but for what would later come to be called "contemporary French thought." At approximately the same time, Jacques Derrida was developing his own, rather similar, reading of Nietzsche, to which he would first make reference at the end of his 1963 essay "Force and signification." Both Deleuze and Derrida foregrounded Nietzsche's thinking about energetics as the antidote to what had become stagnant in the academic schools of phenomenology and structuralism. As a concept, "energy" would seem to belong to an outmoded, nineteenth century way of thinking. Deleuze and Derrida both argued that such was not the case, that metaphors of energy were precisely what was needed to shake up and to destabilize efforts to establish the priority of the metaphysical concept of "structure," and to invent new ways of thinking at the border between psychology and ontology. Derrida (1967/1978) wrote, "In the future, [structuralism] will be interpreted, perhaps, as a relaxation, if not a lapse, of the attention given to *force*, which is the tension of force itself. *Form* fascinates when one no longer has the force to understand force from within itself. That is, to create" (p. 4; emphases in original). Deleuze (1962/1983), more to the point, expressed the same sentiment thus:

> Nietzsche's concept of force is [...] that of a force which is related to another force: in this form force is called will. The will (will to power) is the differential element of force. A conception of the philosophy of the will follows from this. For the will is not exercised

mysteriously on muscles or nerves, still less on 'matter in general', but is necessarily exercised on another will. The real problem is not that of the relation of will to the involuntary but rather of the relation of a will that commands to a will that obeys—that obeys to a greater or lesser extent. (p. 7)

What Deleuze and Derrida both had recognized is that we make a grave mistake if we imagine that Nietzsche insists on multiplying perspectives simply for their own sake, for the purpose of cultivating a beautiful soul in the aesthetic pursuit of "life as literature" (Nehamas, 1985). Rather, perspectivism has a specific—"therapeutic"—function: to neutralize *ressentiment*. In Book I of the autobiographical *Ecce Homo* ("Why I am so Wise") Nietzsche (1887/1989b) writes:

> Freedom from *ressentiment*, enlightenment about *ressentiment*—who knows how much I am indebted, in this respect also, to my protracted sickness! This problem is far from simple: One must have experienced it from strength as well as from weakness. If anything at all must be adduced against being sick and being weak, it is that man's really remedial instinct, his *fighting instinct*, wears out. One cannot get rid of anything, one cannot get over anything—everything hurts. Men and things obtrude too closely; experiences strike one too deeply; memory becomes a festering wound. Sickness itself *is* a kind of *ressentiment*. (pp. 229–230)

So that men and things do not "obtrude too closely," perspectivism is an effort to maintain the "pathos of distance" that figures at the origin of nobility (2003, p. 54; 1887/1989b, p. 26). To achieve noble distance one must have the perspectives of both weak and strong where *ressentiment* is concerned, to have suffered it and to have laughed it off all the more forcefully as a result. Overcome with *ressentiment*, weakness has but one remedy: cultivating the "pathos of distance," what Nietzsche in this passage metaphorically describes as "Russian fatalism":

> [...] that fatalism without revolt which is exemplified by a Russian soldier who, finding a campaign too strenuous, finally lies down in the snow. No longer able to accept anything at all, no longer to take anything, no longer to absorb anything—to cease reacting altogether. (1887/1989b, p. 230)

Taken out of context, such statements again feed the myth of Nietzsche as a proponent of nihilism. In fact, Nietzsche is proposing a form of neutral non-activity intended to redress the balance not of activity and passivity, but of activity and reactivity, in order specifically to defuse reactive modes of nihilistic abandon:

> Because one would use oneself up too quickly if one reacted in any way, one does not react at all any more: this is the logic. Nothing burns one up faster than the affects of *ressentiment*. Anger, patho-logical vulnerability, impotent lust for revenge, thirst for revenge, poison-mixing in any sense—no reaction could be more disadvan-tageous for the exhausted: such affects involve a rapid consumption of nervous energy, a pathological increase of harmful excretions—for example, of the gall bladder into the stomach. *Ressentiment* is what is forbidden *par excellence* for the sick—it is their specific evil—unfortunately also their most natural inclination. (ibid.)

Acknowledging *ressentiment* is forbidden to the weak because it is what reveals their weakness *as* weakness and *not* as strength—that is why it is instead attributed to the motivations of the strong as indication of their "evil." *Ressentiment* weakens and so it must either be discharged through perspectival strength or projected into the other. Such projection is, par-adoxically, the "strength" of resentful weakness, its capacity to over-take affects of command and to proliferate itself, spreading sameness and indifference. This is the origin of the "impotent lust for revenge." Projecting *ressentiment* does not make the weak into the strong but just the opposite, it reinforces sickness and encourages a more insistent cir-cuit of reactive degeneration. "Russian fatalism" is also a metaphor for portraying what Nietzsche elsewhere famously celebrates as the love of fate—*amor fati*—though again it would be wrong to think this beatifi-cally: "Accepting oneself as if fated, not wishing oneself 'different'—that is in such cases *great reason* itself" (p. 231). "Fatalism" is not nihilism but a technical strategy for countering the impulse toward wishing that things were different, that one's life or situation was otherwise, which is precisely the effort of the will to refuse time and finitude—the essence of metaphysics, the becoming-reactive of force. By countering all efforts at merely *wishing* one were different, which amounts to trying to pre-serve sameness against all obstacles (time being the most tenacious), one becomes capable of active differentiation, opening up a hierarchical "distance" between strength and weakness:

> Born of weakness, *ressentiment* is most harmful to the weak them-selves. Conversely, given a rich nature, it is a *superfluous* feeling; mastering this feeling is virtually what proves riches. Whoever knows how seriously my philosophy has pursued the fight against vengefulness and rancor, even into the doctrine of "free will"—the fight against Christianity is merely a special case of this—will understand why I am making such a point of my own behavior, *instinctive sureness* in practice. (Ibid.)

A "rich nature" is perspectival. Perspective is therapeutic in that it makes *ressentiment* a "superfluous condition." Nietzsche is "making such a point of [his] own behavior" to demonstrate this essentially auto-therapeutic character of perspectival truth—its identity with the project of "self-overcoming" as that which "proves riches." Again we encounter the fact that, for Nietzsche, perspective is not to be identi-fied with subjective opinion, nor is it to be opposed to objective fact. Perspective is *"instinctive sureness* in practice"; its purpose is to guide practical activity just as much as positivist facticity, itself a reactive form of interpretation (a "halting before phenomena"). As *"instinc-tive sureness* in practice," perspectivism does not facilitate or expand the space of cognitive self-reflection, but it does enhance the capacity for judgment—and not reflexive judgment that legislates moral action, but unconscious instinctual judgment in the service of life: affirmation. *"Instinctive sureness* in practice" can sound quite worrisome (especially for clinicians), but for Nietzsche this sureness constitutes an uncom-promising "yes"—and not to *a* meaning but to "countless meanings." These meanings do not present themselves "to" a subject that is for-mally distinguishable from and thereby capable of confronting the world; they are articulated *as* states of "instinctive sureness" that give rise not to reflexive self-awareness but to decisive, life-affirming activ-ity, even where such "activity" consists in an apparently "passive" neutrality. "Instinctive sureness" is not conscious certainty; it is the effect of interpretation, not explanation. Interpretation does not reveal underlying meaning; it produces meaning as active, motivating force driven to act on the world-historical scene—that is, the network of all relationships, of commanding and obeying: "This world: A monster of force ..." (Nietzsche, 2003, p. 38).

Revaluation, repetition, technique

In one of the earliest fragments that opens *Daybreak* (1881/1997b), Nietzsche writes:

> What is astonishing in the realm of science is the opposite of what is astonishing in the realm of the conjurer. For the latter wants to persuade us to see a very simple causality where in truth a very complicated causality is at work. Science, on the contrary, compels us to abandon belief in simple causalities precisely where everything seems so easy to comprehend and we are the fools of appearance. The "simplest" things are *very complicated*—a fact at which one can never cease to marvel! (p. 9)

The object of Nietzsche's reproach here is not mysticism ("conjuring"), but contemporary science itself, which remains primitive to the extent that it privileges "a very simple causality" over and above complexity. This is the form of science that Nietzsche otherwise calls positivism, which makes of us "the fools of appearance" because it "halts at phenomena," privileging conscious, explanatory "facts." The science capable of appreciating phenomenal complexity is genealogy. Substituting simple, singular, substantive origins for the complexity of dynamic processes is again among the central gestures of metaphysics.

Soon after this passage, Nietzsche introduces what the subtitle of *Daybreak* has already announced is its central concern: "Thoughts on the prejudices of morality." He begins by asserting that we live today in a thoroughly "immoral age," and that this is because, "the power of custom is astonishingly enfeebled" (p. 10). Whereas in the *Genealogy of Morals* Nietzsche famously begins by deriving the perverse ("weak") framework that distinguishes "good and evil" from the intrinsically "natural" evaluation of the "good and bad," here his starting point lies elsewhere (though it is a crucial point that will be repeated in the later texts). Before having to do with good and evil, and before even having to do with their derivation from a reversal of the intrinsic values of good and bad—that is, before the universal is derived from and subsequently exalted over and above the particular—morality is essentially a matter of establishing custom:

> [...] the *chief proposition*: Morality is nothing other (therefore *no more!*) than obedience to customs, of whatever kind they may be; customs, however, are the *traditional* way of behaving and evaluating. (Ibid.)

Before the establishment of the *content* of moral evaluation (good and evil), morality is nothing but submission to customary *practices*. Repeatedly performing any task opens up the path toward the establishment of tradition as a technical procedure for behaving and for evaluating. This has no relation to moral valuation as such, nothing to do with what is "right" or even what is "useful"; it is simply an effect of practices of mechanical repetition that have become ingrained over time and that establish an irrational reverence:

> What is tradition? A higher authority which one obeys, not because it commands what is *useful* to us, but because it *commands*. —What distinguishes this feeling in the presence of tradition from the feeling of fear in general? It is fear in the presence of a higher intellect which here commands, of an incomprehensible, indefinite power, of something more than personal—there is *superstition* in this fear. (p. 11)

Tradition governs to the extent that it is a source not of ordinary fear but of compulsion in relation to an indefinite power. Deviating from the routine of the traditional puts us at odds with a power that neither threatens nor inspires but that commands. There is nothing intrinsically useful in this obedience; we do not "choose" as rational subjects to obey for the benefit of the effects that will follow. I "know" that certain customs I engage with and experience as meaningful are only forms of repetitive routine, but I am compelled to follow them nonetheless, and despite my intermittent awareness of their emptiness and irrationality:

> Originally all education and care of health, marriage, cure of sickness, agriculture, war, speech and silence, traffic with one another and with the gods belonged within the domain of morality: they demanded one observe prescriptions *without thinking of oneself* as an

individual [...]. Originally, therefore, everything was custom, and whoever wanted to elevate himself above it had to become law-giver and medicine man and a kind of demi-god: that is to say, he had *to make customs*—a dreadful, mortally dangerous thing! (Ibid.)

This is where Nietzsche's project departs dramatically from all forms of Kantian and post-Kantian critique (including that of Freud). In opposition to all discourse on Enlightenment as the modern interpretation of the purpose of "education and care," Nietzsche insists on the priority not of liberation but of "elevation," through a transgressive-creative care-taking of the means of customary procedure or of tradition-production. Why is the effort to make customs "a dreadful, mortally dangerous thing"? This is the mortal danger that the "freethinker" *qua* Enlightened Kantian critic felicitously avoids, but not so the Nietzschean "freedoer":

One has to take back much of the defamation which people have cast upon all those who broke through the spell of a custom by means of a *deed*—in general, they are called criminals. Whoever has overthrown an existing law of custom has hitherto always first been accounted a *bad man*: But when, as did happen, the law could not afterwards be reinstated and this fact was accepted, the predicate gradually changed; —history treats almost exclusively of these *bad men* who subsequently became *good men*! (p. 18)

The figure of the criminal is the interpretation that established tradition inevitably bestows upon the one who inaugurates new forms of tradition—new behaviors and new evaluations—around which the world must gradually and affirmatively reconstitute itself. In this way, that which initially appears as "bad" is retroactively revaluated as "good": The criminal becomes lawgiver, medicine man, demi-god. Nietzsche here keenly intuits crucial aspects of the dynamics of transference. Morality is linked to causality and to agency; together these form a framework for interpretations that govern the horizon of what is historically, experientially possible. Interpretations are not the underlying causal decisions of a moral subject; they reflect organizations of drives or of forces that both integrate and separate self and world as individuating-relational articulations of will to power:

Sense for morality and sense for causality in counteraction. —In the same measure as the sense for causality increases, the extent of the domain of morality decreases: For each time one has understood the necessary effects and has learned how to segregate them from all the accidental effects and incidental consequences (*post hoc*), one has destroyed a countless number of *imaginary causalities* hitherto believed in as the foundations of customs—the real world is much smaller than the imaginary—and each time a piece of anxiety and constraint has vanished from the world, each time too a piece of respect for the authority of custom: Morality as a whole has suffered diminution. He who wants, on the contrary, to augment it must know how to prevent the results from being *subject to control*. (p. 12)

The belief in a clearly discernable and therefore easily manipulable order of simple causal relation erodes all "superstitious" obedience to moral tradition. Causality is a form of interpretation that diminishes the power of tradition—a power that is still capable of appreciating complex origins that command reverence and that program behavior. Where one is no longer capable of appreciating "imaginary causalities"—that is, complex chains of inference that must be *constructed* rather than merely observed as simple, positive fact—accidental effects and incidental consequences no longer appear relevant. The diminution of morality here is a diminution in the experience of meaning or value. A procedural knowledge for producing effects by means of the manipulation of simple causes substitutes for an experience of meaningfully engaging tradition (history). When Nietzsche writes, "He who wants, on the contrary, to augment [history, tradition, meaning] must know how to prevent the results from being *subject to control*," he is indicating that the lawgiver or medicine man (*qua* "criminal") is not the one who refuses history, but who historicizes in a new and altogether different way. Causality—the mechanical relation of cause and effect that dominates the modern scientific interpretation of the world, the origins of which Nietzsche discovers in Christianity, and to the extent that it appropriates Aristotle's interpretation of time as linear, teleological progression—diminishes the power of moral interpretations of the world not because it is their adversary but to the contrary because it distills moral interpretations down to their very essence. Causality is a mechanical interpretation of the world that reveals the essence of morality as technical, mechanical procedure. Modern mechanical science is therefore not the remedy for a moral, religious worldview, but an effort to enforce globally what makes religious interpretation so powerful in the first place. For Nietzsche, religious morality has always been purely technical, based in techniques of repetition; its meaning is not transcendentally but historically grounded. The Newtonian vision of a clockwork universe set in lawful motion is not the enlightened antidote to religious superstition, but the ultimate worship of "a higher intellect which here commands, of an incomprehensible, indefinite power, of something more than personal." This is the perspective of conjurers, not of scientists:

> If the historical drive does not also contain a drive to construct, if the purpose of destroying and clearing is not to allow a future already alive in anticipation to raise its house on the ground thus liberated, if justice alone prevails, then the instinct of creation will be enfeebled and discouraged. (1886/1989a, p. 95)

It is the coordination of these efforts at destruction and construction that Nietzsche calls for here that he will later formulate as "perspectivism"—another name for what he means here by "the instinct of creation"—as a form of science beyond metaphysics. The "historical drive"—the drive to uncover faithfully the facts of the past as an effort at "destroying and clearing" the errors of the present—must contain within itself an unhistorical "drive to construct" that is capable of using error and illusion to the advantage of future life. As Nietzsche makes clear earlier in this passage, "justice" is the scholarly pursuit of factual knowledge confused with the moral good—a truth that appears to *justify* the status quo.

Against the status quo, perspectivism celebrates the advantages of untruth (illusion), uncertainty, and ignorance. As such it is vehemently *anti*-philosophical, where philosophy, since Socrates, has been defined as the pursuit of universal truth as what is intrinsically, supremely valuable on its own terms. The triumph of the Socratic moral valuation of knowledge as inherently good—as against the inherent badness of untruth, ignorance, and illusion—gradually and inevitably engenders the splitting apart of subjective experience and objective fact, ruining capacities to connect individual action up to the cultural, historical world at large: "Thus the individual grows fainthearted and unsure and dares no longer believe in himself: He sinks into his own interior depths" (p. 84). Nietzsche here may be implicitly referring not just to Socrates but to the philosopher Descartes—whose *Meditations* set the stage for the naturalization of the category of the subject, resulting in a world in relation to which Nietzsche's own meditations can only appear "untimely"—though he might equally be anticipating our own contemporary "culture of narcissism" (Lasch, 1979), which he recognizes as having taken root already in his day. What is clear is that nowhere is this "faintheartedness" more in evidence, for Nietzsche, than in what currently passes for philosophy—a castrated image of thought in the form of lifeless, academic scholarship:

> One may think, write, print, speak, teach philosophy—to that point more or less everything is permitted; only in the realm of action, of so-called life, is it otherwise: There only one thing is ever permitted and everything else simply impossible: thus will historical culture have it. Are there still human beings, one then asks oneself, or perhaps only thinking-, writing- and speaking-machines? (Nietzsche, 1873/1997a, p. 85)

At stake in Nietzsche's plea here is the possibility of a new figure of thought—and thus of philosophy, which is to say of science—as life-affirming interpretation. Untruth, error, and illusion would be as intrinsically beneficial for such a practice as truth, where truth is denied any intrinsic moral justification and is subordinated to whatever promotes life as affective, relational complexity. For Nietzsche, real philosophy is more "clinical" than academic, more "therapeutic" than scholarly. Nietzsche's approach to philosophical practice inaugurates an approach to philosophy itself as forceful, relational engagement: the production via words and concepts of effects elaborated directly on the body—affectively as an increase in "strength" rather than cognitively as an increase in understanding: "The error in treatment: One does not want to fight weakness with a *système fortifiant*, but rather with a kind of justification and *moralization*; i.e. with an *interpretation*—" (1968a, pp. 29–30). Where justice and morality are recognized not as facts but forms of interpretation—of a reactive form of interpretation driven to "halt at phenomena"—what is called for is a practice of interpretation beyond the metaphysical opposition of historical and narrative (objective and subjective) truth.

Clinical example

Three years into her analysis, a patient (E) suddenly decides that she wants a psychiatric referral, so that she might obtain a prescription for

Lexipro. She says she is excited by the fact that several of her friends are on it, and she has been very impressed with the commercial advertisements she has seen on television. She insists that in no way does this mean that she intends to stop our working together in analysis. In fact, she says, she doesn't see any connection at all between our work and the anxiety that her professional life causes her, for which she feels she needs medication. Referring to the analysis, E complains, "This takes a long time. I know you believe in analysis as a way of dealing with anxiety, but I need something to help me *right now!* You don't give me any advice ... I need someone who will give a shit ... I need to know what to wear for fashion week in New York!" I told her I would be happy to advise her on what to wear for fashion week, but I wasn't sure what good it would do her. She laughed and requested instead that I read to her at night as she fell asleep, and that I boil a pot of tea for her to wake up to in the morning. When I pointed out that what she was asking for was not advice, but something rather different, she huffed and demanded, "Well, whatever it is, just give me *that!*"

That she might benefit from the ongoing engagement of an analysis could only be experienced by this patient as a complete disappointment. She was frustrated that I wouldn't give her something "useful": pills, advice, love, shit. Many patients similarly express frustration that the analyst won't say what he "really thinks"—that the analyst just interprets, refusing to address them in the way a subject would an object. That this is so disappointing is related to the fact that the clinical situation, again perspectively conceived, does not involve an educative imparting of positive knowledge. E did not want me to interpret her experience; she wanted me to address her as a master would a disciple by giving her an ideal, immediate access to the real underlying cause of her distress. She understood that this is what most other forms of psychotherapy promise, and that even if this promise were completely disingenuous this would be more bearable than the encounter with the analyst as neutral interpreter. That people insistently prefer subservience rather than freedom in this way was always the most central problem for Nietzsche:

> You want, if possible—and there is no more insane "if possible"—
> *to abolish suffering*. And we? It really seems that *we* would rather
> have it higher and worse than ever. Well-being as you understand

it—that is no goal, that seems to us an *end*, a state that soon makes man ridiculous and contemptible—that makes his destruction desirable. (1886/1989a, p. 153)

Today [...] when only the herd animal receives and dispenses honors in Europe, when "equality of rights" could all too easily be changed into equality in violating rights—I mean, into a common war on all that is rare, strange, privileged, the higher man, the higher soul, the higher duty, the higher responsibility, and the abundance of creative power and masterfulness—today the concept of greatness entails being noble, wanting to be by oneself, being able to be different, standing alone and having to live independently. (Ibid., p. 139)

Taking up this problem with regard to the clinic, we could say that, in order to ensure that the analytic process does not degenerate into an advisory relationship, the analyst must guard against the tempting but ultimately irrelevant question as to the cause of the patient's suffering. This is the patient's own question with which he comes to analysis: "Tell me doctor, why am I suffering?" What Freud understood in advocating a position of neutrality is that the analyst must not allow herself to be seduced into making this question her own—that we must refuse the position that Nietzsche saw as occupied by the priest (in clinical terms: the expert who claims to know how the mind ought to work, what one ought to want and how one ought to live). In contrast, the analyst's question must always be not: *Why* is the patient suffering? but: *How* is the patient suffering? What is important is not the cause but the immanent structure of our self-imposed misery—the way we secretly derive pleasure from our suffering at a level that both escapes and determines our conscious self-awareness. This was the revolutionary insight of Freud's early topographical model: The patient consciously suffers because unconsciously he enjoys it. But *how*, in what way does this enjoyment articulate itself? Why does *this* form of suffering appeal to the patient *so much*? What constitutes the specificity of his suffering, and what can it tell us about the singularity of his perspectival experience of the world? Before the advent of psychoanalysis, tending to the singularity of experience in this way, rejecting any consideration of universals in favor of an appreciation of the unusual, the rare, the unpredictable, and the distinct was the essence of Nietzsche's critique of metaphysics.

Clinic

On Nietzsche's account, interpretation does not produce knowledge by coordinating past and present in a way that reveals timeless, universal truth. Interpretation transforms the one who knows, and not by enhancing self-reflective understanding but by modifying hierarchies of force. Nietzsche is a thinker of meaning, differentiation, and relationality. Perspectives are not modes of consciousness capable of reflecting inwardly on themselves, but motivations to action. Multiplying perspectives does not allow one to see the world through a multiplicity of subjective "points of view"; it unconsciously enhances will to power in its relentlessly singular yet ever-evolving determination. Psychology is not, on Nietzsche's account, introspective. One does not "expand awareness" by accumulating perspectives, but just the opposite: By dispensing with the metaphysical notion that there is *a* meaning *behind* phenomena, and by embracing the phenomenal surface of experience as the play of multiple, indeterminable meanings (values), genealogy allows one to overcome obsessive conscious reflection and the order of the concept. This is what it means to say that genealogy is evaluative, that it is a process of selection, rather than a form of archeological memory retrieval. Conceptual thinking or conscious self-reflection issues from and further reinforces the splitting apart of psychology, physiology, culture, and politics. The originality of Nietzsche's perspectival, genealogical approach is to hold these domains together in order to promote a spontaneity of action rather than a more critical, reflective mode of self-awareness. James J. Winchester (1994) expresses this succinctly when he writes, "What sets Nietzsche apart from the tradition is not so much any one revolutionary concept or group of concepts, but a different attitude towards conceptual thinking" (p. 32).

Nietzsche's philosophical concept and practice of perspectivism offers analysts a way of thinking differently about what the clinical practice of interpretation consists in, as distinct from practices of explanation. Explanation, for Nietzsche, is a moral interpretation of interpretation. It rests on the basic assumption that truth is inherently good, and in such a way that identifies truth with factual objectivity. This identity is what Nietzsche calls positivism: the identity of a moral interpretation of truth with the notion of universal, objective fact—a truth that is "good" precisely because, and to the extent that, it can be shared by all. For Nietzsche, factual explanation fails as a properly scientific procedure because phenomenal experience is not something that appears "to" a conscious subject that preexists it or that could exist in isolation from phenomenal experience; rather, phenomenal experience is itself a product of the relation between mind and world, where these are conceived dynamically in terms of unconscious multiples of force or will to power. "Facts" are merely states of consciousness that reduce anxiety by appearing to arrest the flow of becoming (time) and to establish the certainty of positive knowledge as epistemological ground.

For all practical purposes, what this indicates clinically is that where the analyst interprets the patient's experience of the present in terms of the experiences that shape his past (in the analysis of transference, for example), the result can be the achievement of a great deal of "understanding" that serves merely to suppress anxiety in the moment, but that serves no genuinely mutative function over time. It is in the context of such analyses that one so often hears a patient say, "I understand myself so much better now, but still I feel the same ..." For Nietzsche, to gain understanding is not necessarily to introduce perspective, where the latter is conceived as a reorganization of drive forces that give rise to the experience of conscious understanding in the first place. Understanding, on this account, is a possible effect—but not the cause—of therapeutic transformation. In the marketplace of popular therapeutic techniques, psychoanalysis is invariably identified with efforts to produce change by means of self-reflection and understanding, characterized by explaining the present causally in terms of the historical, developmental past. Nietzsche allows us to reconsider whether that is what the practice of interpretation in the context of a repetitive, neutral setting can be reduced to, or whether this metaphysical interpretation of interpretation—which, again, rests on the alleged moral goodness of factual truth—does not in fact prevent us from intervening as effectively as possible against unconscious efforts to refuse difference, becoming, and change.

CHAPTER TWO

Nietzsche, psychoanalysis, individuation

> We know, our *conscience* knows today—*what* those sinister inventions
> of priest and Church are worth, *what end they serve*, with which that
> state of human self-violation has brought about which is capable of
> exciting disgust at the sight of mankind—the concepts "Beyond",
> "Last Judgement", "immortality of the soul", the "soul" itself: They
> are instruments of torture, they are forms of systematic cruelty
> by virtue of which the priest has become master, stays master ... .
> Everyone knows this: *And everyone none the less remains unchanged.*
>
> —Nietzsche, *The Anti-Christ*

In the previous chapter I attempted to demonstrate how Nietzsche's
critique of metaphysics aims at dismantling attachments to certainty, security, and knowledge in order to cultivate individuation as "strength," as against nihilistic tendencies toward the inherent
"weakness" of group identifications that promote "herd mentality."
For Nietzsche, democratic individuality is imitative non-individuation;
genuine individuation requires the agonistic enhancement of differences over and against moral programs that idealize equality in order
to maintain systems of both psychic and social equilibrium. The implicit

37

suggestion of my first chapter, which will be developed throughout this chapter and the chapters that follow, was that psychoanalysis, unlike other forms of treatment, provides a technical framework for this agonistic encounter with hierarchy and difference, rather than a merely supportive, humanistic-interpersonal approach to the other as object:

> Metaphysics is still needed by some, but so is that impetuous *demand for certainty* that today discharges itself in scientific-positivistic form among great masses—the demand that one *wants* by all means something to be firm [...] this is still the demand for foothold, support—in short, the *instinct of weakness* that, to be sure, does not create sundry religions, forms of metaphysics, and convictions but does—preserve them. (Nietzsche, 1882/2001, p. 205)

Popular misconceptions continue to regard Nietzsche as a champion of the strong over and against the weak, in favor of the rule of the elite "Overman" who inspires fear in the cowering masses. This perpetuates the image of Nietzsche as monstrously immoral, while missing entirely the real orientation of his project. Whether ironically or perversely (it depends on one's perspective), Nietzsche delighted in projecting this image of himself and of his thinking in order to provoke this very reaction. In no way did he actually expect a return to Homeric values from out of the morass of contemporary culture (at least, not after his disillusioned break with Wagner). What he did expect was for his writing to be able to shake to its very foundations the world that finds "foothold, support" for itself in the progressivist ideals of positivist science. The one who breaks with these ideals does not thereby ascend to some position of potency or mastery (one can find no better example of small-mindedness than those who would point to Nietzsche's short, tormented life as evidence that his philosophy refutes itself—a small-mindedness that today speaks out against psychoanalysis in the name of "evidence-based treatment"). What is always at issue for Nietzsche is not some given opposition between strength and weakness, but dynamic processes of *becoming*-strong and *becoming*-weak that tend toward imperceptible reversals such that weakness comes to predominate and nihilism becomes the principle of adaptation. What concerns Nietzsche is precisely the fact that the strong are not strong, that the weak are not weak, that health is not adaptive, and that pathology is no longer aberration. As Derrida (2002) insightfully remarks:

As soon as there is reversibility, this principle of inversion, Nietzsche himself cannot prevent the most puny weakness from being at the same time the most vigorous strength [...]. When Nietzsche says that the strong have been made slaves by the weak, this means that the strong are weak, that Nietzsche comes to the rescue of the strong because they are weaker than the weak. In a certain sense, by coming to the aid of strength, Nietzsche is coming to the aid of weakness, of an essential weakness. (p. 226)

This "essential weakness" is nothing less than will to power as the essence of processes of individuation or of becoming-active. It is what makes Nietzsche's anti-moral campaign more ethical than slave morality is capable of grasping. When Nietzsche describes "the demand that one *wants* by all means something to be firm" as the "instinct of weakness" itself, what is implied is that what is strong in strength is its essential infirmity, a radical openness and sensitivity beyond empathy for the other figured as object (it is out of strength that Nietzsche collapses in Turin at the sight of an animal being abused). The "pathos of distance" that defines the condition of "nobility" is not rooted in disdain or contempt but just the opposite (1887/1989b, p. 37). Nietzsche sees that everywhere social relations are composed of non- or pre-moral techniques of individuation and regression: relations of force that command or that obey, and that in doing so produce more or less complexity and affective engagement. It is in this light that we must think what Nietzsche has to teach psychoanalysis today: "Variation, whether as deviation (to something higher, subtler, rarer) or as degeneration and monstrosity, suddenly appears on the scene in the greatest abundance and magnificence; the individual dares to be individual and different" (1887/1989a, p. 211). If we read him in the way that he demands to be read—with great care—Nietzsche can be a tremendous resource in the efforts of psychoanalysis to bring about such daringness both within its clinic and in the world at large as it relates to the clinic.

A horse is being beaten

The book that inaugurates Nietzsche's "mature" period, and in which he first elaborates key themes that will inspire his most famous works, is also the most neglected of his texts, even in the scholarly literature: *Daybreak: Thoughts on the Prejudices of Morality* (1881/1997b). This text introduces the elementary conceptual matrix that links together Nietzsche's critique of morality with his critique of causal logic and his critique of the illusion of subjective agency. These three critiques are inseparable; any attempt to isolate the insights of one from the domains of the other two inevitably leads to misapprehension. Though it is not without good reason that *Daybreak* has been overshadowed by the more literarily austere *Beyond Good and Evil* and the more argumentatively rigorous *Genealogy of Morals*, efforts to make sense of the force of Nietzsche's critical projects in those texts must begin by taking into account their predecessor.

At the end of the preface to *Daybreak*, Nietzsche makes a comment intended to orient the reader not only in reading this text but in reading those that follow and that build on its themes (he will repeat exactly the same sentiment in the final section of his preface to the *Genealogy of Morals*). He writes:

> It is not for nothing that I have been a philologist, perhaps I am a philologist still, that is to say, *a teacher of slow reading*: —in the end I also write slowly. Nowadays it is not only my habit, it is also my taste—a malicious taste, perhaps? —no longer to write anything which does not *reduce to despair every sort of man who is "in a hurry"*. For philology is that venerable art which demands of its votaries one thing above all: to go aside, *to take time, to become still, to become slow*—it is a goldsmith's art and connoisseurship of the word which has nothing but delicate, cautious work to do and achieves nothing if it does not achieve it *lento*. But for precisely this reason it is more necessary than ever today, by precisely this means does it entice and enchant us the most, in the midst of an age of "work", that is to say, of hurry, of indecent and perspiring haste, which wants to "get everything done" at once [...]. (1881/1997b, p. 5; emphases modified)

Daybreak was first published in 1881. This statement was written for its rerelease, during the autumn of 1886—a period when Nietzsche was most certainly not in the habit of writing slowly. This was a time of furious production in Nietzsche's life that would culminate in his collapse less than three years later. Yet this should not dissuade us from taking him at his word when he describes himself as a "teacher of slow reading" whose "malicious" intention is to "reduce to despair" those ignoble readers who are increasingly incapable of taking time, becoming still. Nietzsche is passing judgment upon the pathologies of his age, which he had already foreseen and demonstrated against during the period of the text's original production:

> *Fundamental idea of a commercial culture.* —Today one can see coming into existence the culture of a society in which *commerce* is as much the soul as personal contest was with the ancient Greeks and as war, victory and justice were for the Romans. The man engaged in commerce understands how to appraise everything without having made it, and to appraise it *according to the needs of the consumer,* not according to his own needs; "who and how many will consume this?" is his question of questions. This type of appraisal he then applies instinctively and all the time: He applies it to everything, and thus also to the production of the arts and sciences, of thinkers, scholars, artists, statesmen, peoples and parties, of the entire age: In regard to everything that is made he inquires after supply and demand *in order to determine the value of a thing in his own eyes.* This becomes the character of an entire culture, thought through in the minutest and subtlest detail and imprinted in every will and every faculty: It is this of which you men of the coming century will be proud [...]. (p. 106)

It is against the background of this sentiment that we should read Nietzsche's efforts at a "revaluation of all values." In attempting such a revaluation—what is also, if less famously, here called "the re-education of the human race" (p. 13)—Nietzsche is not reacting against the spirit of his age but working just as furiously and productively alongside of it, in order to push efforts at revaluating already underway in different directions. Commercialism is primarily, for Nietzsche, not an economic but an interpretive practice—a practice of evaluating, comparing, fixing, and determining—one figured by a tremendous speed (which is to say, a liberation of drives) the likes of which the world has never seen before. To teach *slow reading, taking time* and *becoming still* today is an effort not only to resist this form of interpretation—interpretation performed not just *for* but *by* the "needs of the consumer"—but to interpret otherwise, according to other needs, affects, and desires.

In an early text entitled, "On the uses and disadvantages of history for life," collected among his *Untimely Meditations* (1873–1875/1997a),

Nietzsche examines the obsession of his age with accumulating facts about the historical past. Although he does not name it as such, this essay contains the origins of what he would later go on to develop as "perspectivism." The academic accumulation of historical details is double-edged for Nietzsche. While it may promote investment in the health of contemporary culture by drawing on the resources of the past in the search for "strong" (for the young Nietzsche: Hellenic) ideals, it may just as equally suffocate openness to future possibility by substituting historical positivism for cultural inventiveness:

> We want to serve history only to the extent that history serves life: for it is possible to value the study of history to such a degree that life become stunted and degenerate—a phenomenon we are now forced to acknowledge, painful though it may be, in the face of certain striking symptoms of our age. (p. 59)

The "striking symptoms of our age" that Nietzsche refers to are contained in what he diagnoses as the essentially unhistorical, non-narrative character of contemporary life. Turned toward the past in an effort to discover the meaning of historical processes, toward which the current age is alleged to be advancing, what was once historical culture subordinates life to the liberal pursuit of "advanced" scientific knowledge. The accumulation of knowledge is confused with the cultivation of life: "[...] with an excess of history man ceases to exist" (p. 64). That is, the human ceases to exist historically, becoming incapable of historical action or decision, accepting more and more that the way things are is the way that they ought to be:

> [...] in this rumbling there is betrayed the most characteristic quality of modern man: the remarkable antithesis between *an interior which fails to correspond to any exterior and an exterior which fails to correspond to any interior*—an antithesis unknown to the peoples of earlier times [...] This precisely is why our modern culture is not a living thing: It is incomprehensible without recourse to that antithesis; it is not a real culture at all but only a kind of knowledge of culture; it has an idea of and feeling for culture but no true cultural achievement emerges from them. (p. 78; emphasis added)

On this account, the modern world consists essentially in a relentless splitting apart of self and environment, expressed as the opposition between subjectivity and objectivity that drives the marketplace of modern technological science. It is, to use a psychoanalytic vocabulary (Deutsch, 1942), an "as-if" culture—a culture that pretends to knowledge of its past, but only in the form of an accumulation of factual details that have no bearing on the living articulation of the present. For Nietzsche, this is an historically unprecedented event that gathers all forms of modern culture together under the general heading of nihilism. Nihilism follows on the predominance of what Nietzsche here calls, "the blind powers of the actual" (1873–1875/1997a, p. 106). The "actual" names this lack of coordination that produces a sense of interiority which finds nothing to connect itself up to in the external world. The result is investment in traumatic overstimulation, normativized self-hatred, and paralyses of creativity:

> To speak without euphemism: The mass of influx is so great, the strange, barbaric and violent things that press upon the youthful soul do so with such overwhelming power that its only refuge is an *intentional stupidity*. Where there has been a stronger and more subtle awareness, another emotion has no doubt also appeared: disgust. The young man has become so homeless and doubts all concepts and all customs. (p. 98; emphasis added)

It would be difficult to find a more presciently accurate description of our own age by a writer working almost 150 years ago. By invoking stupidity, Nietzsche is not being basely provocative or arrogant; he is identifying a very real psychological and socio-political problem that produces the most devastating historical consequences, as several critics have begun to elaborate upon today (Ronell, 2002; Derrida 2008/2009; Stiegler, 2006/2013, 2012/2015). Stupidity here is not the absence of cognitive intelligence, but a will to self-destructiveness that masquerades as knowledge, self-confidence, and strength. "Intentional stupidity" might be thought as, "to be stupid intentionally" (to be actively self-destructive), as much as, "to be stupid in one's intentions" (to be passively self-destructive). Either way, this has become the default position of those overwhelmed by environmental demand, by the proliferation of *i*-objects, by efforts to undermine their ability to inherit an experience of historical continuity under massive conditions of adolescent "Attention Deficit Disorder." Youthful disgust with the adult world— less and less in evidence these days, as already for Nietzsche—at the very least manifests a healthy attitude of rebelliousness and a desire for change. Nietzsche sees that in the modern period it is this last figure of consciousness that is being swallowed up and destroyed, with the result that the only form the expression of creativity can finally assume is an unbridled destructiveness (Columbine, Dunblane, Utøya, and so on) as an anticipatory stage to the triumph of apathetic conformity.

The comparison of what Nietzsche describes with Helene Deutsch's influential concept of the "as-if personality" is not fortuitous. What psychoanalysis has struggled to understand in terms of the clinical phenomenon of "as-ifness" was anticipated by Nietzsche in his thinking about nihilism, weakness, and morality. Deutsch's as-if personality is one who demands explanation in the place of interpretation, and who allows us further to appreciate and to develop the differences between these two clinical modalities as outlined in the previous chapter. What Deutsch and the literature that has followed in the wake of her contribution describe at the level of individual psychopathology, Nietzsche had warned of as threatening the horizon of contemporary culture and civilization.

Knowledge

Famous for its introduction of the concept of the "as-if personality," Deutsch's 1942 paper is less memorably entitled, "Some forms of emotional disturbance and their relationship to schizophrenia." What is indicated is a form of pathology that is not properly neurotic, yet only "related" to psychosis—neither neurotic nor psychotic, but indicative of an intermediary position that would seem to link the one to the other. This is a way of saying that patients such as these confound classical psychoanalytic thinking about the relationship between neurosis and psychosis, because they force us to reconsider not only diagnostic categories but our thinking about the relationship between mind and world. Such patients present a condition in which, "the individual's emotional relationship to the outside world and to his own ego appears impoverished or absent" (p. 301). Deutsch is disturbed by these patients who satisfy criteria for socially adaptive behavior, but who manifest something that strangely does not quite "fit":

> [...] every attempt to understand the way of feeling and manner of
> life of this type forces on the observer the inescapable impression

that the individual's whole relationship to life has something about it which is lacking in genuineness and yet outwardly runs along "as if" it were complete [...] There is nothing to suggest any kind of disorder, behavior is not unusual, intellectual abilities appear unimpaired, emotional expressions are well ordered and appropriate [...]. But despite all this, something intangible and indefinable obtrudes between the person and his fellows and invariably gives rise to the question, "What is wrong?" (p. 302)

To say that, "There is nothing to suggest any kind of disorder," save for the fact that something seems "wrong" with the patient's "whole relationship to life," is to run up against a clinical difficulty that implicates psychoanalytic thinking itself, especially where it attempts to draw clear distinctions between the normal and the pathological. The analyst who expects to serve as a source of identifications for the purpose of strengthening the adaptive capacities of their patients' egos will find these patients particularly frustrating and incomprehensible. The as-if personality simultaneously requests and refuses individuation, by imitating identifications rather than by forming them. The result is a form of treatment that is at once as stagnant as it is potentially endless. Grasping "what is wrong" is singularly difficult for analysts who— either consciously or unconsciously—conceive of clinical practice as dedicated to promoting normative adaptation through increased self-awareness. It seems as if self-awareness is precisely what these patients lack, although they are possessed of a strong capacity to present as if this were not the case. It is not clear if one is dealing with an absence of self-awareness, or with a strange form of hyper-self-awareness whose function it is to isolate the patient from "life." The sense one receives is that one is engaged with an "automaton" (p. 305). This is why Deutsch situates this condition somewhere between neurosis and psychosis: Adaptation is present, but self-awareness is not. The as-if patient is an "automaton" to the extent that he or she is socially integrated and possessed of reality testing, yet essentially lacking where "genuineness" is concerned. Where psychoanalysis is conceived of as oriented toward understanding as an increase in the ability to engage in self-reflection, it has difficulty accounting for those patients who appear to demonstrate this capacity, but as a way of fending off the possibility of difference. The as-if patient is perfectly possessed of the ability to pursue understanding, but for this very reason nothing ever moves the clinical dialogue forward. Understanding functions as the obstacle that prevents, rather than the vehicle that invites, therapeutic change.

Deutsch writes, "[...] the emotional disturbance may be perceived as existing in the personality or it may be projected onto the outside world" (p. 301). That is, these patients may present as aware that something is "wrong" with them, or they may just as easily regard the world itself as at fault. More generally one finds oscillation between these two perspectives: The patient alternately complains of the uniqueness of his individual suffering at his own hands, and of the world as a Kafkaesque bureaucracy implicitly designed to prevent him from getting ahead. The former claim often seems designed to communicate to the analyst that self-understanding is being generated when in fact it has a distinctly unreal quality, while the latter claim seems designed as a plea to persuade the analyst to agree with the patient that the world is not the place it ideally ought to be. Either the as-if individual suffers from feeling incapable of connecting up to the world at large, or from an experience of the world itself as lacking in invitations to connect. Deutsch explains this by stating rather categorically that, "Psychoanalysis discloses that in the 'as if' individual it is no longer an act of repression but a real loss of object cathexis" (p. 304). The "real loss" indicated by the inescapable disingenuousness of the as-if individual produces as a result the feeling in the analyst that, "all inner experience is excluded. It is like the performance of an actor who is technically well trained but who lacks the necessary spark to make his impersonations true to life" (p. 303).

What Deutsch refers to as the "necessary spark" intrinsic to "life" may seem intuitively coherent, but it is more difficult to define conceptually. If we situate the essay in its historical context, it is clear that Deutsch in 1942 is appealing to a popular discourse that had its roots in Nietzsche's work. The term *lebensphilosophie* was current as a reflection of the critique of Enlightenment rationalism, as expressed in the writings of Schopenhauer, Kierkegaard, and above all, Nietzsche. It is no accident that Deutsch appeals to the terms of this discourse in her attempt at describing the as-if individual (the reference to Vaihinger at the opening of the essay is enough to indicate that Nietzsche is not far from her mind). Positivism, in Nietzsche's sense of the term, is precisely what these pseudo-individuals demand in the everyday clinical encounter: explanatory reductions of experience to unambiguous conscious fact. What Deutsch describes as an unusual clinical syndrome,

Nietzsche had already described as, "the most characteristic quality of modern man: the remarkable antithesis between *an interior which fails to correspond to any exterior and an exterior which fails to correspond to any interior*—an antithesis unknown to the peoples of earlier times." For Nietzsche, modernity—defined by its commitment to the accumulation of factual knowledge and the deformation of its "relationship to life"—*is* this very condition that Deutsch recognizes defies psychoanalytic commonsense. Nietzsche's critique of Darwinism had always stressed the extent to which adaptation can itself be a pathological condition, serving the interests of the "weak" rather than the "strong." A psychoanalysis that emphasizes normative adaptation will always find cases such as the ones Deutsch describes disconcerting, and not only because they resist classical forms of clinical intervention, but because they indicate how normal behavior can itself function as a form of severe psychopathology. The analyst who prides himself on being authoritatively "healthy" can only be deeply unsettled when confronted with patients who demonstrate this very condition yet without providing a sense of their being "truly alive."

It is crucial to Deutsch's approach that the as-if individual not perceive what others find so unnerving about him. Although later commentators (e.g., Ross, 1967; Roshco, 1967) would attempt to expand the concept of the as-if personality to include those who experience intense feelings of emptiness and who report all manner of existential crises (what would generally fall under the heading of narcissistic self-pathology today), Deutsch is consistent about the patient's lack of perception—the lack of "genuineness" even when lip service is paid to such perception—as to where the difficulty actually lies (hence her astonishment at the "real loss of object cathexis"). This is what gives the clinical work its uncanny "automation"-like quality, as an encounter with someone who is not authentically individuated. With the as-if individual, it appears *as if one is dealing with an individual,* but the shallowness and lability of identifications, the lack of genuine affect, and the absence of capacities for transformative self-observation indicate that one is not. Chris Mawson (2004) poignantly writes, "I see 'as-if' personalities as individuals who have not been able to limit themselves to forming defensive structures *in* their minds, but have become single-mindedly devoted to making defensive structures *of* their minds" (p. 521; emphases in original). When working clinically with such patients, the temptation towards acting out on the part of the analyst is powerful due to the frustration that ensues on the patient's commitment to remaining in treatment while using the analyst's interpretations to ensure that nothing actually happens. In a potentially endless treatment without change, automatism substitutes for autonomy. As a result, the analyst is drawn to abandon a neutral-interpretive stance in favor of a humanistic appeal to "genuineness." In Nietzsche's terms: Where Being is idealized over becoming, the pull towards countertransferential boundary violation indicates the reactive becoming-weak of the active force of analytic neutrality.

Clinical example

A struggling actor in his forties (R) has chronic problems with debt and supplements his meager income by shoplifting. He seems self-reflective enough that over time we are able to develop the idea that his going into debt is a way of forcing others to take care of him. Beyond this, we understand his behavior as a way of forcing others into a position where he can test whether they will indeed take care of him or abandon him, as he felt his father had when he was a child. Together we are able to stay with this idea, and to explore how this behavior manifests itself in several different situations in his life, particularly in his relationship with his landlord. The landlord has not received a check for a full month's rent from the patient for the several years. R seems able to incorporate an understanding of how he uses this present relationship to negotiate the difficulties that continue to haunt him from his childhood. Nevertheless, each month ends with the patient's claim that despite what he has come to understand about himself, he knows that this time his failure to have the month's rent will provoke his landlord to throw him out on the street. For years the landlord has turned a blind eye, telling R not to worry. In other words, the landlord has passed the test with flying colors. And yet, each month R and I find ourselves managing his anxieties about being homeless. After these episodes he always understands how his childhood anxieties and disappointments were activated once again, and how this seems to happen every month. But this insight is invariably washed away each time his rent check is due, for this time, he always insists, things are different. *This time* it's not about his fantasies, he *really is* going to be thrown out on the street, despite all evidence that nothing distinguishes this time from episodes in the past. When overcome by these anxieties, as far as he is concerned, there is nothing to interpret, he *knows* what is going to happen to him if he does not come up with the money to pay his rent.

R is politically engaged and spends much time in treatment telling me about the injustices he witnesses in the world. He has suffered financial difficulties his entire life, but he is able to organize these difficulties into, "the fact that I'm working class." R was raised by a single mother who worked two jobs in order to ensure that her children would have the opportunity to go to college. He had pursued this opportunity, but had dropped out a semester before graduation. Years later his mother suffered a stroke, which R blames on her employers for having "worked her to the bone." His mother's condition is evidence to him of how unjust the world is, of how the rich get richer and the poor get poorer. Repeatedly he assures me, "I really believe what Noam Chomsky is saying." When I point out that Noam Chomsky nevertheless makes a fair amount of money believing as he does, R is dismissive. His problems are ultimately political, he explains, adding, "I can't be neurotic, I'm working class."

Eventually R is able to confide in me a thought he has been contemplating for years but that he has quietly kept to himself. This is his discovery that, "the Jews run the world." There follows, of course, much talk about whether I take offence at this statement, about his inability to decide whether or not I am Jewish, about psychoanalysis being a "Jewish science," and about how these things impact on the transference. But, he insists, this is not anti-Semitism, he is simply describing that, "the Jews really do run things." Over time and with much apparently good work we come to discover that this was a belief instilled in him by his mother, and that now he unconsciously blames these people for having destroyed his mother. Eventually R is able to understand that by keeping himself in poverty, he is fighting these mysterious enemies. Later he even considers that the relationship between his mother and "the Jews" represents his own relationship with his mother and the suffering he felt under her direction but which he has difficulty acknowledging. This is all very impressive to him, and he claims that it helps him to make sense of the bizarre incongruity he now perceives between his radical liberalism and what he considers an inherited anti-Semitism. However, one conviction remains unchanged by all this: "The Jews really do run the world." This, he continues to insist, is not objectively in and of itself a strange or biased idea.

There was no questioning what R *knew* to be *true*. He repeatedly *knew* that his landlord would throw him out of his apartment, despite all evidence to the contrary, and despite developing an apparent ability to reflect on the unconscious determinations of his anxieties. Later he discovered how inconsonant it was for him to hold a belief that was so at odds with his general ideological commitments. Reflecting on this allowed him to understand that his past experiences with his mother had influenced and continued to influence the thoughts and opinions he held to this day. It did not, however, change the *fact* that he *knew* he was *right*, and that this was not a matter of prejudice or perspective, it was simply, innocently *true*.

One can imagine the extent to which working with such a patient elicits a degree of frustration that begins to approximate what Winnicott (1949) described as "hate in the counter-transference," and with Nietzsche and Deutsch one might wonder whether that is not precisely the intention of the symptom as something the patient does not suffer from but "projects onto the world." These were not typical instances of the tenacity of neurotic symptoms, and R was certainly not psychotic, although his symptoms had the quality of unmodifiable, psychotic delusion. In the analysis, R appeared to demonstrate genuine shifts in his ability to reflect on his experience of himself, but clearly this was not the case—or rather, even if it were the case, it didn't make any difference, as the underlying ideas to which he was committed—what he presented as *knowledge* of how things *simply are* (what Nietzsche called metaphysics)—remained immune to change.

Non-knowledge

Winnicott's essay "The location of cultural experience" opens with a quotation from the poet Tagore: "On the seashore of endless worlds, children play." He goes on to reflect:

> The quotation from Tagore has always intrigued me. In my adolescence I had no idea what it could mean, but it found a place in me, and its imprint has not faded. When I first became a Freudian I *knew* what it meant. The sea and the shore represented endless intercourse between man and woman, and the child emerged from this union to have a brief moment before becoming in turn an adult or parent. Then, as a student of unconscious symbolism, I *knew* (one

always *knows*) that the sea is the mother, and on to the seashore the
child is born [...]. (1971, p. 95, emphases in original)

Although the account is offered anecdotally, it contains an important
insight that runs throughout Winnicott's work. His sense of *knowing*
reflects a defensive organization of experience that refuses to recognize
any perspective beyond the momentary identification of consciousness
with immediate perception. *Knowing* is an experience of knowledge
as eternal, timeless truth—metaphysics. One always *knows* in that one
always knows, where knowledge has the character of timeless revelation
or of universal objectivity. *Knowing* describes an emergent experience
of self identified with reality as presence (Being). What is left unac-
counted for is the fact that knowledge evolves and is transformed over
time (becoming), that knowledge is not the accumulation of facts but
an active capacity for interpretive (perspectival) self-transformation.
In the clinical example cited, the patient seemed to acquire new ways
of reflecting on himself, yet nothing essentially changed. This was certainly not an instance of repression, which operates *through* symbolic
processes by effecting disguised substitutions for inadmissible desires.
But does this reflect the emergence of organized self-states that fail to
register their incongruity with the rest of self-experience, or does it indicate a kind of defense that operates *on* symbolic processes by denying
that experience is symbolically mediated? Do R's convictions depict
radically dissociated self-states embodying the "knowledge" he insists
upon, or does his insistence on such "knowledge" indicate a defensive
collapse of the symbolic links that would allow him to interpret and to
assume responsibility for his experience? In asserting that "the Jews run
the world," R was not unaware of his anti-Semitism, rather he was unaware of it *as* anti-Semitism—as interpretation—because his claims felt
so plainly, objectively self-evident. Instead of keeping this idea out of
consciousness, he had become so insistently aware of it that it became
something that was for him clearly real and so not in need of being
reflected upon or interpreted, despite its obvious incompatibility with
who he presented himself as and believed himself to be.

We always *know* before we realize that we don't know, before having taken the time to realize that there are other ways of thinking and
understanding and knowing about things. *Knowing* is a pathology of
certitude. It insists that what is actual and real is only what I can see
before me or factually understand right now. For Nietzsche, this is

another form of valorizing consciousness and local causal relations; it is opposed to what Freedman (1998; Freedman & Lavender, 2002; Lasky, 2002) called "symbolization" as an ability to tolerate the emergence of different ways of experiencing. Defense against symbolization—what Freedman called "desymbolization," which involves being closed to the course of time, over which other perspectives might emerge and take the place of, without erasing, current perspectives—organizes time as ideal presence, as the absolute reality of the *here-and-now*.

Interpretation intrinsically challenges this position. When we interpret patients' symptoms, we are demonstrating that certain things they experience and that they think mean one thing can also mean another. The phobic anxieties of a patient who cannot tolerate the sight of certain animals, for instance, are revealed through analysis to symbolize parental intercourse. The animals are not just animals, they represent not only themselves, they are intrinsically differentiated from themselves in ways that are not immediately, perceptually apparent but that remain concealed: They *also* mean *at the same time* something else entirely. Interpretation discloses meaning as difference. As a therapeutic technique, interpretation is based on the assumption that the patient can tolerate that experience might be meaningful in ways that are not readily apparent. Clearly, however, there are cases in which this assumption is not justified, in which the contingency of perceived truths is itself intolerable, and in such a way that has nothing yet to do with their symbolic content. This contingency is the heart of Nietzsche's perspectivism, and it is what the "positivistic" attitude of the as-if individual cannot account for. As Deutsch herself indicates, where this intolerance is not a global condition that defines either the clinical relationship or the patient's "whole relationship to life," we still find instances of this attitude in the course of any ordinary analysis. These are instances in which *what* the symbol stands for is not the problem; rather it is the fact *that* symbols represent something else than they appear to depict on the conscious, perceptual surface that is so difficult.

The ability to tolerate that reality might not be what it immediately appears to be is the defining feature of a symbolizing attitude. Hanna Segal (1994) distinguishes, "between concrete symbolism, in which the symbol is equated with what is being symbolized, and a more evolved form, in which the symbol represents the object but is not confused and identified with it, and does not lose its own characteristics" (p. 396). This "more evolved form" involves openness to other possibilities for experiencing oneself in relation to the environment, where environment is tolerably imbued with the capacity for change—a non-metaphysical experience of environment as temporal becoming and not as subordinate to the intransigent fantasy of some unchanging, eternal truth or "good." This openness is another way to conceive of symbolization. Thomas Ogden (1986) writes, "Understanding the meaning of one's experience is possible only when one thing can stand for another, without *being* the other; that is what constitutes the attainment of symbol formation" (pp. 218–219; emphasis added). With the adoption of a symbolizing attitude, one thing can always stand for another, but it is not equivalent to that which it represents. The as-if individual—in the same manner as the psychotic, yet without compromising adaptation to "reality" (again, the source of Deutsch's consternation)—insists on equivalences that collapse the differentiating function at the heart of a symbolizing attitude. The clinical relationship as a result manifests an unremitting sameness that screens out what Nietzsche had called, "the dangerous 'maybe'" (1886/1989a, p. 11).

Reversibility

Ruth Riesenberg Malcolm (1992) integrates Deutsch's concept of the as-if individual with Bion's thinking in order to describe what she calls "the phenomenon of not learning"—again calling attention to the fact that what is at issue is a peculiar relation to knowledge (recall that for Nietzsche "revaluation" is "re-education"—to educate the uneducable is to overcome nihilism). She expands Deutsch's thinking in ways that further approximate Nietzsche's understanding of the "intentional stupidity" that defines contemporary commercial culture:

> This way of functioning aims at keeping an appearance of an analysis in progress, while the patient's main objective will be to keep the situation immobilized. A static situation acts for these people as a kind of reassurance, a kind of proof that they are all right, do not need any change, which they prove by perceiving themselves endowed with keen analytic perceptions and gifts and rich emotions. (p. 114)

By stating that, "a static situation acts for these people as a kind of reassurance," Malcolm offers a way of thinking as-ifness dynamically, as a phenomenon rather than as a diagnostic entity rooted in developmental, environmental deprivation. What is "static" (eternal) provides "reassurance." This is what Nietzsche describes as the essence of metaphysics: The certainty of causality, unity, and Being substitutes for the risk of anxiety-provoking non-knowledge intrinsic to a "Dionysian" confrontation with becoming (chance, change, time, difference). The as-if patient insists on positive, factual "knowledge" in an effort precisely not to learn or to develop. Analysis becomes a way of ensuring static immobility because, "The patient's equilibrium is threatened by life" (p. 115).

Malcolm builds on what Bion, in his slim but dense volume, *Elements of Psycho-Analysis* (1963/1984b), calls "reversible perspective." Bion names this with reference to the famous figure-ground illusion in which one perceives either a white vase or two black faces turned towards one another. It is possible to see either one or the other figure represented in the image, but not both at the same time. In order to shift from one figure to the other, one must "reverse" one's perspective while still looking at the same picture. The analogy here is to a clinical situation in which, "analyst and analysand appear to be speaking the same language, to have many points of agreement and yet to remain without any tie other than that of the mechanical fact of continued attendance at analytic sessions" (p. 49). This is a situation in which analyst and patient are in total agreement about the "facts"—that an analysis is indicated, that it is in the process of being conducted, that interpretation serves to provide understanding in the context of transference as repetition—but in such a way that guarantees nothing but immobility. There is agreement but no "intersection" (p. 51) between the perspective of the patient and the perspective of the analyst. As Malcolm (1992) describes, "Patient and analyst, though appearing to be together, do not make contact. It is precisely the contacting link which is cut, leaving the interpretation useless, repetitious, and empty" (p. 123).

Bion is famous for having been extraordinarily attuned to the nuances of primitive mental states, but the phenomenon he is describing does not belong to psychosis. It has to do rather with a psychical structure that is itself externalized and imposed on the clinical relationship, in which the patient oscillates between knowledge and non-knowledge—in Bion's algebraic terms, "between K and –K":

> The significance of the agreement between analyst and patient
> lies in the fact that the agreement is obvious and obtrusive but

the disagreement, which may be just as obtrusive, is by no means obvious. It lies in the use of the agreed facts by the patient to deny what he is convinced are the facts. The conflict between the view of the patient and analyst, and in the patient himself, is not therefore a conflict, as we see it in the neuroses, between one set of ideas and another, but between K and minus K (–K) or, to express it pic-torially between Tiresias and Oedipus, not Oedipus and Laius. (1963/1984b, p. 51)

Like the faces and vase of the figure-ground illusion, analyst and patient are observing the very same phenomena, but their perspectives could not be more at odds—and not in a way that produces dynamic conflict but in a way that seems strangely, irresolvably integrated yet fastidi-ously opposed. Unlike the conflict between Oedipus and Laius, this is not a conflict that can be resolved where one vanquishes the perspec-tive of the other—this is not a typical neurotic transference that calls for a dialectical approach to how reality is to be understood. Rather, like the conflict between Oedipus and Tiresias, this is a situation in which the participants both see and are blind to aspects of reality, but in com-pletely different and opposing ways, the result of which can only be an endless, futile power struggle. Bion writes:

> The common-sense view of mental development is that it con-sists in an increase of capacity to grasp reality and a decrease in the obstructive force of illusions. Psycho-analysts suppose that the exposure of archaic phantasies to modification by a sophisticated capacity for approximation to a series of theories, that are consistent and compatible with the reception and integration of further expe-rience, is therapeutic in its effects. This supposition cannot stand up to rigorous examination, but has to be received with indulgence to receive meaning of value. (Ibid.)

This is an extraordinary statement from 1963. Bion is challenging the predominant approach to psychoanalysis as a practice that promotes adaptation by furthering allegedly inherent processes of development towards the acceptance of "common-sense" reality. He specifically cau-tions that any such teleological, developmental thinking in psychoa-nalysis compromises its status as science. Any technique that relies on communicating to the patient psychoanalytic theories of development as a measure of what maturity consists in "has to be received with indulgence to receive meaning of value." Where the patient is incapable of such indulgence—incapable of encountering an axiological "meaning of value"—efforts on the part of the analyst to explain the patient to himself reflect fantasies on the part of psychoanalysis itself about what "reality" consists in. This is the lesson Bion draws from patients who present an insistently "reversible perspective"—neither classically neurotic nor psychotic—who insist on an appreciation of "facts" as the measure of reality in order to constitute a "contact barrier" that protects from the influence of the analyst as potential for transformation and difference:

> Clinically the picture presented is curiously baffling. There is usu-
> ally no doubt about the severity of the patient's disability, but it is
> difficult even for the patient to say why he seeks analysis. It may
> also be possible at first to underestimate the degree of severity of
> disturbance. But before long the lack of contact between analyst
> and patient and the lack of signs of ordinary conflict begin to build
> up an unmistakable picture. There is evidence that the patient is
> prey to extremely painful emotional experiences: The analyst usu-
> ally has to rely on the patient's report as the only evidence of these.
> If they take place in the session the patient invariably has a fac-
> ile "explanation" of what is taking place. The explanation is often
> couched in terms that successfully disguise the real nature of the
> experience. If the patient has been in analysis for some time they
> are manipulated in such a way that they invite interpretation in
> terms that the patient has learned to expect from the analyst—the
> "agreed" intersection is thus maintained. Between analyst and
> patient there is thus established what I have elsewhere called a
> contact barrier. (pp. 52–53)

"Agreement" constitutes a "contact barrier" that both connects and divides in a thoroughly static way. Analyst and patient are factically in agreement with one another as to the problems in the patient's life that are to be "solved," but in such a way that there is no exchange between individual perspectives. As should only be expected, the patient seeks help for his suffering, which the analyst agrees to dedicate herself to helping to alleviate. This constitutes the "mechanical tie of attendance" to the schedule of analytic sessions, such that an analysis seems to be occurring. The patient regularly attends the sessions, speaks, listens and responds to what the analyst has to say. But what emerges is a clinical picture in which the demand for help is met with a dedication that screens out the possibility of actual transformation because it thinks in terms of adaptation to reality conceived of in oppositional, subject/object terms, which is precisely what the patient is courting so as to deny otherness and difference as real possibilities:

> The model of reversible perspective, when applied to the analysis, reveals a complex situation. The patient detects a note of satisfaction in the analyst's voice and responds in a tone conveying dejection. (What was said is irrelevant to our immediate concern.) The patient detects a moral supposition in an interpretation: His response is significant for its silent rejection of the moral supposition. That which makes one person see two faces and the other a vase remains insensible, but in the domain of sense impressions there is agreement. The interpretation is accepted, but the premises have been rejected and others silently substituted. (p. 54)

Bion is here at his most subtle and incisive, challenging classical analytic expectations about the intrinsic connections between interpretation, knowledge, and therapeutic action. He is describing the moment-to-moment interactions of a patient and analyst couple that has been reduced to attending solely to the "mechanical" dimension of the analytic process—the neutrality of the frame. When he writes, "The patient detects a moral supposition in an interpretation: His response is significant for its silent rejection of the moral supposition," he is describing how the analyst's interpretations are experienced as if they were intended to pass judgment, to indicate that what the patient is saying is "wrong." This is countered with a "silent rejection of the moral supposition"—the patient does not protest the analyst's perceived condemnation but rather accepts that moral opposition is the very form of the analytic relationship itself as a relation between a subject and an object. By "moral supposition" Bion does not mean that the analyst is experienced in the transference as the externalized embodiment of the patient's superego. Rather, the "moral supposition" at work is the patient's assumption that the analyst is merely someone with his or her own subjective perception that—because it is "merely subjective"—can easily be either accepted or refused without consequence. The "atmosphere of morality" here is encapsulated by the patient's cool, agreeable insistence that the analyst's interpretations are superficially appreciated, but easily dismissible because they represent only someone else's subjective "opinion." Malcolm too emphasizes the "atmosphere of morality" attendant on these cases, in which, "the analyst has vague feelings of guilt, sometimes mingled with irritation and despondency" (1992, p. 116). The patient's response to the analyst's interventions is typically prefaced by conditions such as, "I understand what you mean, but the way I see it ..." or, "You're right about that, but still ..." or, "I hadn't thought of that, and I also think. ..." The "atmosphere of morality" elaborates itself as if the clinical relationship were merely a democratic dialogue in which patient and analyst thoughtfully compare perspectives and calmly agree either to agree or to disagree. As Nietzsche describes, morality consists here in the imposition of a subject/object structure of opposition that neutralizes genuine affective engagement. A detached judgment as to whether interpretations are right or wrong prevails. Perspectives are "reversible" to the extent that they are not experienced as perspectival in Nietzsche's sense (as interpretations of the course of time—for Nietzsche, interpretation does not engage facts but time or becoming as such), but as collections of opinions considered as contained subjective realities competing with but not fundamentally open to one another. "Reversible perspective" is an attempt to insist on Being (as eternal presence) over and against the influx of becoming: Something either *is* subjective or objective, right or wrong, good or evil, black or white.

Clinical example

The patient described above who believed that the world was run by a conspiracy (R) began a session by complaining that it was difficult for him to meet that day of the week, and that he would prefer to reschedule that day's appointment regularly to another day. This was the second time he had voiced this complaint. On the previous occasion, I had offered him the opportunity to begin meeting on the day he said was preferable. He had said he would think about it, so I asked him if he had thought about it. He said he had not, that he still needed time to think the decision through. I continued to ask him about this, why he felt it would take him time to think through what seemed to be a relatively simple decision, given his complaints. When he dismissed my inquiries, I commented that it seemed to be something he was not comfortable thinking through with me, but which he preferred to think through by himself. Suddenly, with exasperation he accused me of "playing mind games," and of not letting him go on to talk about more important topics with which he had been preoccupied. When I asked him what he thought my motivations might be for "playing mind games," he became all the more frustrated and said that he was now beginning to wonder if I wasn't pushing him to take the other hour, since that would be more convenient for me, and that as a result I had wasted several minutes of his session by pressing him about what was essentially my own issue with our rescheduling. There was some degree of truth to what he was saying, so I relented in my questioning and thought instead about how my countertransferential feelings, of which I had not been aware, had influenced my interventions.

Relieved that I had "finally dropped it," R went on to talk about "what was really bothering him." Since our last meeting, which he said had affected him greatly, he had spent much time soul searching, trying to answer the question as to what had happened to him as a child to have damaged him so badly as an adult. He listed several childhood events—the death of a parent, the introduction of an abusive stepparent, intermittent poverty—all of which had certainly been terribly difficult for him. With each scenario intended to explain his current condition, he asked me what I thought, did it make sense? Since our sessions often followed this formula, I told him that I thought what might be worth our looking at was his interest in my opinion as to whether what he had come up with about himself was "correct." Annoyed that I would not answer him by just telling him what I thought, he recalled a previous analyst who had been forthcoming with interpretations linking his present to his past, and how helpful this had been. He then spent the rest of the session wondering whether not just I, but psychoanalysis itself, could ever really be of help.

This patient wanted me to interpret how the past events of his life determined his present feelings and behavior, in such a way that would help him make sense of his current problems. Which of these past traumatic events, he would repeatedly ask me, do you think makes my present condition comprehensible? This is certainly not an unreasonable request for a patient coming for psychodynamic treatment to make. But our sessions often became a caricature of the therapeutic process: R would tell me about things that happened to him in his childhood, and I was supposed to point to one and say, "Aha! Now everything makes sense, you see?" It seemed to me rather that by focusing on the past events of his life, and by not so subtly trying to coerce me into doing the same by invoking a previous analyst, he was insistently trying to draw both of our attentions away from what was clearly going on in the clinical moment: that he was in control, and that reflection on anything besides the material that he was consciously intending to present would not be tolerated.

This was also what had happened earlier in the session around the possibility of our rescheduling. Here the patient insistently did not want me to interpret his indecisiveness. It was after all just an issue of scheduling, nothing more complex than that, and why would I not let it go? To R, the scheduling issue had no meaning; to suggest that it might have symbolic meaning was to be "playing mind games."

In both instances, although in one the patient seemed to be refusing interpretation, while in the other he seemed to be demanding it, the important point was that he was in control of the outcome whichever way our struggle fell: Either I could interpret according to rules that he had spent his time since the previous session deciding, or I could not interpret at all. I had also succumbed to this logic with regard to the issue of our rescheduling appointments: In becoming preoccupied with the possibility that my unconscious ideas and feelings about our rescheduling had pushed me to interpret his indecisiveness, I lost sight of the fact that even if this were true, it would not have interfered with the interpretation that I had offered. That is, even if my behavior had been determined countertransferentially, this did not necessarily mean that his behavior was not a figure of the transference. By assuming that these possibilities were opposed to one another, I had adopted the patient's way of organizing the experience of our working together: either I was right or he was right, either transference was real or countertransference was real, either one could interpret or one could not. From R's perspective, it did not actually matter which one of us was right or wrong; what was important was that neither one of us questioned our remaining within the rigid framework of this logical opposition. Interpreting in such a way that attempted to shift beyond this logic was experienced as threatening: If something means both itself and something else, one of us is "playing mind games." At an earlier point in the treatment, and again with reference to Noam Chomsky, R had referred to the "pure power hierarchy" between himself as patient and me as analyst, and now I knew what he meant: the difference between either he or I having control over the immediacy of the clinical encounter.

This patient wanted me to "interpret" his symptoms not in such a way as to open up new perspectives on his experience, but in order to establish a one-to-one correspondence between his current behavior and past events in his childhood. This would in effect provide a kind of magical formula that would render further investigation unnecessary—a causal explanation. His present situation was perceived as statically given, completely determined by remote past events. At the same time, and indeed as a result, there was no real commerce between past and present that would help him come to terms with the ways in which his past continued to repeat itself. Both present and past were experienced in the form of isolated "nows" defined in opposition rather than in relation to one another, so that between them he could only hope to discover some direct, instantaneous connection. Past and present were conceived on the model of simple, singular instants, rather than as complex dimensions of experience in dynamic integration. By refusing interpretations he did not control, R was able to insist that his present was passively determined by his past (a fact over which he often expressed resentment), rather than acknowledge the ways in which he actively shaped his present to conform to his past. This was a patient who in his spare time would consult DSM-IV as a way of trying to understand himself. In instances like the one described above, he used the treatment similarly as an index of possibilities for self-diagnosis, rather than as an opportunity for individuation.

Disavowal

Bass (2000), like McDougall (1980), considers this situation to reflect a defensive repudiation of the differences between patient and analyst as these are revealed through interpretation and the assumption of neutrality. "Concrete" patients, or "anti-analysands," who attempt to reduce the therapeutic relationship to an endless power struggle over who is in control of the "now" (Being) are responding to the inherently tension-raising nature of psychodynamic treatment as a process that unfolds indefinitely over time (becoming), and which makes use of that process of unfolding in the form of the transference as it develops and is interpreted. These patients cannot tolerate the analyst's efforts to open inner experience up via interpretation of the symbolic. Rigid structures of binary opposition—either an interpretation is right or wrong, either you are in control or I am in control, etc.—are imposed on the treatment as a way of ensuring that no progress is ever made. Whether the patient does or does not "win"—whether he or the analyst is in control at any particular moment—is ultimately irrelevant. Narcissistic desires for power and control are sated in the translation of the difference between the analyst's and the patient's perspectives into opposition, since opposition ensures that even if power is lost, it can always be strategically regained. Nietzsche had associated this uncreative, competitive effort with the "weakness" of "commercial culture" as a form of "slave morality."

In "The as-if patient and the as-if analyst" (2007), Bass provides a close reading of Deutsch's original 1942 paper in order to demonstrate how the clinical encounter with the as-if individual can provoke the analyst to abandon neutrality and to favor a conception of the empathic relationship as intrinsically mutative where efforts at interpretation repeatedly fail. By emphasizing the enactments that attend to Deutsch's treatment of the patients she seeks to describe, Bass demonstrates how the as-if patient cultivates an as-if analysis by courting the analyst to abandon the analytic frame in favor of egregious boundary violations that appear justified according to an ordinary moral logic of intersubjective, empathic support. What is disconcertingly "automaton-like" about as-if phenomena draws the analyst into humanistic efforts at interpersonal supportiveness, because the stance of analytic neutrality itself comes to appear similarly "inhuman" in a way that seems to point to its being the source of what is clinically ineffective. Empathy, neutrality, and interpretation are in this way split apart. The "maternal" aspects of analytic care are emphasized over and against the alleged ordinary "paternalism" of interpretive neutrality. Bass criticizes this perceived opposition between analytic interpretation and the analytic relationship common to Deutsch, Winnicott, Balint, and so many others (although there is no mention of it in the text, Kohut's work would seem emblematic of such a split). He argues instead that neutrality makes the analyst into a function of the clinical environment itself as intrinsically interpretive, to the extent that it facilitates the internalization of individuating, differential tensions that promote the development of psychic space necessary for cultivating a symbolizing attitude.

Although relatively brief and presented as an overview both of Deutsch's contribution and of the perspectives of other authors in the field, "The as-if patient and the as-if analyst" reads as a summary statement concerning the author's own contributions in the companion volumes *Difference and Disavowal: The Trauma of Eros* (2000) and *Interpretation and Difference: The Strangeness of Care* (2006), the latter having appeared just a year earlier. In the first volume, Bass outlines the confounding clinical problem of "concreteness" as resistance to interpretation in patients who nevertheless seek out and remain committed to coming for analytic treatment. Concrete patients come to analysis for an interpretive practice but spend their time in analysis subtly repudiating all of the analyst's interventions. Surveying the analytic literature from Freud to Loewald, Bass thinks this situation as a defensive repudiation of the temporally differentiating function of the analytic environment itself, as this is embodied by the analyst's assumption of interpretive neutrality. He links this to what he reads as Freud's late turn to the concept of disavowal to describe the mechanism basic to all compromise formation.

Disavowal indicates the simultaneous registration and repudiation of processive, differentiating aspects of reality. This leads to a psychological state in which the patient can both know and not know something at the same time. This is not a successful integration of knowing and not-knowing that would open up onto anxiety-provoking yet active developmental processes, but a state of eternally (reactively) "oscillating" structures of logical opposition that serve as forms of global, narcissistic defense. The prototypical instance of such a position is that of the fetishist, who oscillates between "knowing" that women are not castrated, and acting *as if* castration were real. The fetishist's attitude with respect to sexual difference is what Bion describes as "reversible perspective." The concrete patient brings this attitude to the analysis as a way of "fetishizing" the analytic relationship itself, in order to avoid interpretation as an ongoing process, again as embodied by the analyst herself in conjunction with the repetitive, "mechanical" nature of analytic treatment (coming to the same place, at the same time, day after day, etc.). The analyst's interpretations are treated as fragmented objects—units of ideation, subjective opinions, "mere perspectives"—rather than as aspects of an ongoing process that both discloses and constructs symbolic meaning. Reversible perspective or concreteness refuses perspectivism as interpretive, individuating-relational becoming; it refuses the technical conditions for creating new forms of tradition. Disavowal registers and repudiates finite time as what commands.

Bass sees in what Bion had called the "mechanical tie of attendance" the key to understanding why such patients would seek out analysis in the first place. It is not the content of the analyst's interpretations that the concrete patient is refusing, but the interpretive process itself as a relationship that promotes individuation by agonistically raising tension levels and that therefore must be split off. As Deutsch might have said, these are patients whose "whole relationship to analysis" is strangely distorted—strange because although they refuse therapeutic possibility based on insight and understanding, they nevertheless remain committed to analysis while insisting upon stagnation. Anxiety related to the repetitive "mechanical tie" not to the analyst as object but to the act of attending the sessions themselves is what the patient is attempting to eliminate by making sure nothing happens, that no matter what is talked about each session remains essentially, disconcertingly the same. This is the "agreement" that Bion had described as a "contact barrier" concealing a more subtle and profound disagreement about what the analysis is intended to achieve. Drawing centrally on the work of Hans Loewald (the argument is repeated at the end of "The as-if patient and the as-if analyst"), Bass argues that the analyst's assumption of neutrality as a form of individuating self-otherness generates in the patient the capacity for a symbolizing (perspectival) attitude when the analytic relationship is internalized, and that this is what the concrete patient is specifically reacting against: the connection to an auto-differentiating other that threatens to provoke processes of individuation–differentiation within the patient him- or herself. The analyst is instead regarded as an authority figure whose authority, because it is experienced as subjectively closed in on itself, can be easily dismissed. The concrete patient comes for analysis but reduces interpretation to a form of interpersonal counseling in order to avoid the traumatically differentiating separation-connection of what Freud had called "Eros."

Where Bass differs from Loewald's approach is in arguing that the difference in organizational "levels" between patient and analyst is not that between the patient's and the analyst's psychic structures. This is a difficult yet crucial point. It is not because the analyst is more psychologically "healthy" or more "normal" than the patient, who is expected to be by definition more pathological, that analysis can be conceived of as facilitating internalization and as opening up the psychic space of self-reflection. It is the analyst's assumption of the neutral-interpretive stance itself that accounts for the difference in structural "levels." Of course, in order to maintain such a technical stance and not be drawn into countertransferential enactments, the analyst must be operating at a structurally sophisticated level of psychic organization. But this does not mean that analysts are to be without psychological conflicts or temptations towards enactment, or that the absence of such conflicts and temptations will inherently promote transformative self-observation when neutrality is abandoned. The analyst who falls back on her own capacity for "genuineness" in order to draw the as-if patient out of his own lack thereof is getting caught up in the power struggle that the patient imposes and that turns the analytic relationship into an endless, ineffectual dialogue. Outside the clinical encounter, such recourse can only appear as moral commonsense. What promotes therapeutic change, however, is independent of what can be demonstrated outside the enduring space and time of the clinic. This has nothing to do with any special status of psychoanalysis itself, but with the singularity of each individual clinical process.

Nietzsche had praised the capacity for "protracted sickness." Concerning *ressentiment* he writes, "This problem is far from simple: One must have experienced it from strength as well as from weakness" (1887/1989b, p. 229). To resist the pull toward countertransferential enactments, which can be thought of as dedifferentiating effects of *ressentiment* in the context of the clinical relationship, one must be capable of experiencing their force. The ability to do so is what Nietzsche calls "strength." It is not enough to self-reflectively "know" that one is being drawn into the patient's efforts at "enactive remembering" (Loewald, 1980, p. 164), as if such knowledge would automatically provide a position of authority and knowledge from which one might correct the patient's distortions. The analyst must both "know" and "not know" that this is what is happening, but not in such a way that opposes these conditions "reversibly." To think reversibly, concretely, or metaphysically is to refuse a form of relational intimacy that has nothing yet to do with empathy conceived as mutual understanding, because it concerns an experience of mind as something prior to—and in excess of—the opposition of self and world.

For this reason, interpretive neutrality should not appear as the opposite of an empathic, supportive clinical approach, but as a more rigorous commitment to individuating-differential openness than clinical approaches that insist on thinking in subject/object terms are capable of appreciating. The encounter with the analyst who maintains a position of neutral-interpretive difference is not an encounter with a "genuine" individual in the ordinary sense (recall the patient cited above who became frustrated that I would not "just tell him what I thought," or the patient from the previous chapter who despaired over the fact that I would not just give her advice). Neutrality means that the analyst does not behave in the clinical setting like a normal individual—that is, as a subject would behave in its ordinary relations to objects. Despite the warmth that the analyst may exude, neutral interpretation always involves a kind of "automaton-like" quality. The analyst as uncanny technical-neutral-interpreter, embodying the interpretive process and in doing so merging with the mechanical, repetitive aspects of the analytic frame, is what the concrete patient avoids by treating the clinical relationship as if it were nothing more than a democratic dialogue between intrinsically opposed subjects who appear to one another fetishistically in the form of objects.

Nobility

In the previous chapter I made reference to the "pathos of distance" that Nietzsche situates at the origin of a "noble" attitude. What this attitude consists in can help clarify what is specific to a neutral-interpretive clinical approach in comparison with other forms of treatment. The opening paragraph of Book Nine of *Beyond Good and Evil* ("What is noble") states:

> Every enhancement of the type "man" has so far been the work of an aristocratic society—and it will be so again and again—a society that believes in the long ladder of an order and rank and differences in value between man and man, and that needs slavery in some sense or other. Without that *pathos of distance* which grows out of the ingrained difference between strata—when the ruling caste constantly looks afar and looks down upon subjects and instruments and just as constantly practices obedience and command, keeping down and keeping at a distance—that other, more mysterious pathos could not have grown up either—the craving for an ever new widening of distances within the soul itself, the development of ever higher, rarer, more remote, further-stretching, more comprehensive states—in brief, simply the enhancement of

the type "man," the continual "self-overcoming of man," to use a
moral formula in a supra-moral sense. (1886/1989a, p. 201)

Those lacking in the capacity for "slow reading" will reactively find this
passage repugnant for its references to aristocracy, slavery, obedience,
and keeping down. In the paragraph that follows Nietzsche warns us,
"not to yield to humanitarian illusions [...] truth is hard." He is not,
however, suggesting that a hierarchical society of masters and slaves is
a reality to which we must assent, that this is the natural state of affairs
in a "healthy" social order. When Nietzsche speaks of the "self-overcoming of man" as a "moral formula" which he intends in a "supra-
moral sense," he means that self-overcoming is not to be construed as
an effort at moral purification by seeking after truth, but as an effort
at "purifying" ourselves of morality—rigid oppositions between right
and wrong, truth and illusion, etc.—as such, in order to engender, "an
ever new widening of distances within the soul itself, the development
of ever higher, rarer, more remote, further-stretching, more comprehen-
sive states." It is not a question of regressing from democracy to the
division between aristocracy and enslavement, but of creating within
contemporary democratic cultures spaces for cultivating that "more
mysterious form of pathos" that generates meaning and tradition. The
psychoanalytic clinic functions potentially as just such a space, and perhaps that is why it faces so much repudiation, both from within and
from without.

   As-if, concrete patients deploy reversible perspective in order to
refuse the "ever new widening of distances within the soul" that
emerges from neutral, individuating-relational engagement. They cannot tolerate the encounter with another person as anything more than
a static, manipulable object. They are enamored of authority figures
with whom they can readily both identify and dispense. They are, in
Nietzsche's sense, weak. It is important to recall here that although
the analytic literature has tended to treat as-if phenomena as a specific
diagnostic entity—as a personality type—it is more generally accepted
that the as-if personality reflects in an encompassing way a phenomenon that one encounters at some point and to varying degrees in any
analytic treatment. Nietzsche, because he spent a lifetime meditating
on this condition, both in himself and in the world at large, provides us
with a way of thinking the emergence of this phenomenon and how to

treat it clinically in terms of the dynamics of the becoming-reactive and becoming-active of force, of weakness and of strength.

The practice of analytic neutrality must be reclaimed from the model of cold, "blank screen" depersonalization. From a perspective informed by Nietzsche's thinking, psychoanalytic neutrality appears "more empathic" than empathy conceived as humanist, intersubjective relation, because it maintains a differentiating, "noble" distance from the other by insistently deferring equality and agreement, opening up the potential for symbolization by means of interpretation and perspective. For Nietzsche, interpretation is thoroughly agonistic, but not mindlessly competitive. The essential weakness of strength, as what makes strength strong in that it is weaker than weakness—as relationally open rather than oppositionally closed—describes the capacity to maintain technical, interpretive neutrality as dependent upon a sensitivity to the other that exceeds all commonsense, metaphysical approaches to empathy as what links subjects and objects together under the sign of some eternal, moral "good."

Finally, the proximity of Nietzsche and psychoanalysis on the question of the as-if personality—those who lack the "necessary spark" of life but who are unable to recognize that something is wrong, and who refuse to learn anything about this condition—raises a much larger, more disturbing question. This has to do with the prevalence of this kind of thoughtlessness outside the clinic. According to Ross (1967):

> It is, indeed, possible that in actual life, "as if" personalities are far more common than in clinical practice. With the lack of insight and deficient affect and the adaptive efficacy of this condition, it is difficult to see what would motivate them to come to treatment. (p. 62)

Nietzsche's *Zarathustra* warns, "The desert grows, and woe to him who conceals the desert within." The phrase recalls Thoreau's (1854/2003) famous line, "The mass of men lead lives of quiet desperation" (p. 11). Citing Nietzsche's words in his 1951–1952 seminar course, published as *What is Called Thinking?*, Heidegger (1954/1968) states, "these are words issuing from thought. They are true words" (p. 38), adding that they come from, "the West's last thinker" (p. 46). As-if phenomena subsume the place of thought where "genuine"—that is, symbolic—thinking has been foreclosed. Where encounters with as-ifness generally predominate, this indicates the extent to which such conditions define a culture that approaches and judges clinical practice in an intrinsically concrete and desymbolizing way. Perhaps there is in this a way of thinking through the crisis of psychoanalysis today, its having fallen out of favor given the demands for cognitive, pharmaceutical, and other "evidence-based," "results-oriented" interventions modeled on, "'work', that is to say, of hurry, of indecent and perspiring haste, which wants to 'get everything done' at once [...]" (Nietzsche, 1881/1997b, p. 5). If psycho-analysis as a discipline cannot adapt to imperative demands for new forms of quick and easy adaptation, analysts might begin to think their orientation otherwise: towards individuation rather than integration, even if this involves more difference, more solitude, and more suffering when confronted with the casual self-destructiveness encouraged eve-rywhere by the pervasive nihilism of contemporary culture.

CHAPTER THREE

Projective identification from Nietzsche to Klein

Every Angel is terror.

—Rilke, *Duino Elegies*

This chapter attempts to put Nietzsche's philosophical project into dialogue with certain aspects of contemporary Kleinian and post-Kleinian thought. In her biography of Klein, Phyllis Grosskurth (1977, p. 17) indicates that as a young woman Klein had encountered Nietzsche's work, but no reference to Nietzsche can be found in her mature writings. Nevertheless, Nietzsche's genealogy of morality strikingly foreshadows Klein's portrayal of the infant's phenomenological world. More specifically, Klein's concept of projective identification powerfully brings to life Nietzsche's insights in a clinical context, and her reflections on envy and gratitude bear a distinct resonance with Nietzsche's critique of bad conscience, nihilism, and *ressentiment*. By demonstrating how Nietzsche anticipated some of Klein's most central contributions, I attempt to use Klein to bring Nietzsche further to bear on clinical concerns, while using Nietzsche to bring out the neglected yet profound philosophical depth of Klein's approach to understanding primitive psychological processes.

Truth, power, pity

In discussing will to power in *Beyond Good and Evil* (1886/1989a), Nietzsche writes:

> "Freedom of the will"—that is the expression for the complex state of delight of the person exercising volition, who commands and at the same time identifies himself with the executor of the order— who, as such, enjoys also the triumph over obstacles, but thinks within himself that it was really his will that overcame them [...] *L'effet c'est moi.* (p. 26)

I am the effect. Among the central "prejudices of the philosophers" of which Nietzsche is critical is "faith in opposite values" (p. 10). One of the effects of this faith is a perceived opposition between free will and determinism: *either* we are free, *or* we are not. The overall strategy of Nietzsche's project is to subvert what makes these alternatives seem so natural in their apparent opposition by arguing that a concept of the will cannot be subordinated to the alleged freedom of a subject, but rather the reverse: The freedom of a subject is not to be measured by the effectiveness of its will. Instead, the freedom of the will is to be indexed by the effects of subjectivity that it is capable of producing.

Beyond Good and Evil begins with the question, "*What* in us really wants 'truth'?" If there is a will to truth that operates in human experience—a will that is expressed most explicitly in the project of philosophy—what is it in us that would correspond to the demand that such a desire be satisfied? What is the *value* of such a will? Why is truth something that carries the assumption of its being intrinsically good and desirable? "*Why not rather* untruth? and uncertainty? even ignorance?" Until Nietzsche, this question had not yet even been posed, much less elevated to the status of a problem: "The problem of the value of truth came before us—or was it we who came before the problem? Who of us is Oedipus here? Who the Sphinx? It is a rendezvous, it seems, of questions and question marks" (1886/1989a, p. 9).

The proliferation of questions and question marks indicated here distinguishes a familiar level of experience from something generally unfamiliar—something Nietzsche will call "unphilosophical." Philosophy asks questions; it is able to do so because it grounds itself in the figure of the self or subject which stands firmly opposed to, so as to be capable of interrogating, the objectively real. By asking after the *value* of truth, Nietzsche is asking about the status of meaning as such. At what stage or from what position is it decided that meaning is intrinsically meaningful? What in us asks after meaning, rather than non-meaning and non-sense, and why? This is what is at issue in the statement, "The problem of the value of truth came before us—or was it we who came before the problem?" What is the position of the subject prior to the inherence of meaning? "Who of us is Oedipus here? Who the Sphinx?" It is no exaggeration to say that Nietzsche is asking philosophy to think in terms of what psychoanalysis calls the pre-oedipal: primitive experience in which self-identity has yet to be fixed or decided, where the positions of interrogator and interrogated—self and other—incessantly undergo reversal and distortion. So at what point, Nietzsche asks, is it decided that meaning is positively meaningful and worth pursuing to its ultimate end? What contributes to this determination if, originally, the positions of Oedipus and Sphinx—subject and world—devolve into one another interminably?

It is with respect to these reversals that Nietzsche posits his concept of will to power. As I discussed in the first chapter, will to power, when read carefully, is anything but a will to exercise domination over others; rather it names a state of cultivated vulnerability from which the world can be experienced as intensely as is possible. Such a will, which Nietzsche insists is not the will of an underlying self or subject, is properly nothing—not a thing, an object—and therefore meaningless, in that it makes the difference between meaning and non-meaning, sense and non-sense, possible in the first place. That is, for Nietzsche, what makes meaning possible is itself meaningless—and yet, it is not simply arbitrary. This is precisely what the concept of will to power attempts to illuminate. Experience is ultimately without meaning, or rather without *a* meaning; all is chance, randomness, flux—*but this is no accident*. Prior to any stable distinction between self and other, in terms of which some ultimate meaning or value might derive, there is still yet an effort to distinguish, to decide between existence and non-existence. This difference is itself without meaning; it can be neither appreciated nor appropriated by a traditional logic that Nietzsche thinks as philosophical "prejudice"—the "superstition of logicians" (1886/1989a, p. 24), "faith in oppositional values" (p. 10).

In his commentary on will to power, Alexander Nehamas (1985) writes that it "is manifested in the ability to make one's own view of the world and one's own values the very world and values in which and by which others live" (p. 32). This is true, but it leaves us dangerously close to the worst misinterpretations. Will to power implies a world shaping force, but not one that is transacted at the level of intersubjective relations. Nietzsche situates will to power at a level where the *inter*personal and the *intra*personal have yet to be clearly distinguished. Classically, the concept of the will has been used to explain the causal link between decision and action, mind and body: *First* there is me, *then* I exercise *my* will to carry out the actions that I command. Nietzsche is constantly at pains to dissociate himself from this erroneous understanding. The priority of the subject with respect to the will must be reversed: It is not that first there is me, and then there is "my" will; rather first there is the will in its pre-subjective, differential multiplicity, and from out of that play of forces emerges a subjective state of self-awareness that is subsequently driven to posit itself retroactively as cause, origin, or ground. Will to power is "a complex of sensation and thinking," prior to any formal distinction between thought and sensation. Will to power is in this sense an affect, "and specifically the affect of command. That which is termed 'freedom of the will' is essentially the affect of superiority in relation to him who must obey" (Nietzsche, 1886/1989a, p. 25). Will to power has nothing to do with traditional discourses on freedom, which is the privilege of a subject; it is an affective, bodily experience, from out of which the conditions of subjectivity arise. *L'effet c'est le moi*—the sense of "having" a self, or being an "I" is a residue, a remainder, not a cause of our activity within the world.

In developing this position, Nietzsche invites us to a kind of thinking that he explicitly deems "unphilosophical": "Let us for once be more cautious," he writes, again in *Beyond Good and Evil*, "[...] let us be 'unphilosophical'"—unphilosophical because he assigns priority to the body and to affect, rather than to consciousness or reason—"let us say that in all willing there is, first, a plurality of sensations, namely, the state '*away from which,*' the sensation of the state '*towards which,*' the sensations of this '*from*' and '*towards*' themselves, and then also an accompanying muscular sensation, which, even without our putting into motion 'arms and legs,' begins its action by force of habit as soon as we 'will' anything" (ibid.).

At the most elementary level, will to power is constituted as a differential of force that develops in terms of the states "away from" and "towards." Away from and towards what? For Nietzsche, that is precisely the question to be avoided, as it is determined by a pathological compulsion to seek after substantive, singular origins. "Will to power" describes instead an irreducible plurality where "towards" and "away" designate pure potentialities, pure movements or displacements of force that need no further justification by being grounded in an underlying point of reference. The play of "towards" and "away" reflects the contours of the will—of strong and weak wills, both between and within organisms (p. 29)—in its tendency towards discharge in the affect of command: "A living thing seeks above all to *discharge* its strength—life itself is will to power; self-preservation is only one of the indirect and most frequent results" (p. 21).

For Nietzsche then, will to power names the capacity to produce effects of subjectivity or selfhood—transitory, discontinuous, contradictory—while prioritizing moments of inspiration in the search for ever more intensive experiences. This is will to power in its positive aspect. With what Nietzsche, in the *Genealogy of Morals* (1887/1989b), calls the "slave revolt in morality"—that is, the emergence of Christianity, as a form of "Platonism for 'the people'" (1886/1989a, p. 2)—will to power assumes a new historical figure that abandons any concern for affective complexity in favor of an ascetic puritanism, and that exchanges a concern with subjective multiplicity through direct action for the production of alienated singularity, interiority, and "bad conscience" in the field of the other. That is, if what Nietzsche calls the "strong" is that which is capable of joyously discharging its strength, the "weak" is that which is not so capable, and which as a result substitutes negativity and destructiveness for enthusiasm and worldly engagement.

One would imagine that Nietzsche contradicts himself by positing the intrinsic value of strength over and against weakness while at the same time denouncing metaphysics as "faith in opposite values." This fails to appreciate that strength and weakness are, for Nietzsche, not essences but themselves forms of interpretation:

> *Weakness of the will*: that is a metaphor that can prove misleading. For there is no will, and consequently neither a strong nor a weak will. The multitude and disgregation of impulses and the lack of any systematic order among them result in a "weak will"; their coordination under a single predominant impulse results in a "strong will": In the first case it is the oscillation and the lack

of gravity; in the latter, the precision and clarity of the direction. (1968a, pp. 28–29)

Strictly speaking, there are no "strong" and "weak" wills, but only will to power existing at different levels of organization. What is weak in weakness is disorganization at the level of the drives, while what is strong in strength is organization under a "single predominant impulse" that commands. In anticipation of my argument in the next section of this chapter, it is worth noting that in this brief passage Nietzsche defines weakness in terms of its tendency toward "oscillation." In Chapter Two, I discussed oscillation as the central feature of Bion's concept of reversible perspective, and of Bass's approach to Freud's concept of disavowal. For Klein, structurally dedifferentiated, paranoid-schizoid functioning always relies on oscillating logics of opposition (good/bad, inside/outside, introjection/projection, etc.). For Nietzsche, oscillation characterizes metaphysics as what integrates oppositional thinking with efforts to deny the existence of time or becoming. Oscillation is a primitive form of psychic containment that maintains equilibrium by reactively insisting on what appears immediately apparent as reflecting what is actually real. This is the "positivism" of Deutsch's "as if personality" as the absence of "the necessary spark" intrinsic to "life"; it is the psychological origin and historical power of the concept of "eternity." Where there is no symptomatic fixation on eternity there is the capacity for mourning, for tolerating loss as a source of tradition and renewal. What Nietzsche calls the "precision and clarity of the direction" of the "strong" would in this sense approximate what in Kleinian terms is described as depressive position integration.

In the *Genealogy of Morals*, the relationship between "strength" and "weakness" is presented in terms of the values assigned by the Christian tradition to pity and to forgiveness. What are we doing when we pity someone? It doesn't sound like such a bad thing: We feel sorry for another person. Nietzsche sees that something much more is at stake. Pity is not a correlate, but rather the opposite of empathy: When I empathize with another, I can, metaphorically, "put myself in their place"—or, more precisely, I can take them into myself ("my place") in a way that establishes a connection—while at the same time sustaining the difference between our states of internal and affective self-awareness. You've suffered the loss of someone dear to you? I can empathize, I can feel sorrow too—*with* you. Pity suggests something else. When I pity you, you don't necessarily feel bad, but I feel bad *for* you, where you seem incapable of feeling bad, as it is thus implied you should. In pitying, I put myself in the place of the other in a much more literal and concrete sense, and the other, as a result, becomes displaced, and begins to feel bad too, like me. So when I can exercise empathy, this means that I can share in the inevitable fortune and suffering of others, whereas pity is thoroughly negative: The other cannot see how much he *ought* to suffer, and this only increases how bad both he and I *must* feel. Empathy would be a discharge of strength, in Nietzsche's sense, whereas pity would not—which is not to say that pity does not produce effects (and affects) of command and subordination. To the contrary, it produces these rather powerfully, albeit in the form of a mutually engendered, rather than deflected, servitude.

In the *Genealogy of Morals*, this understanding of the interpersonal yet pre-subjective structure of pity is developed through an historical analysis of the cardinal Christian virtue of forgiveness. What is forgiveness? Again, for Nietzsche, not what we typically imagine. In one of the most memorable images in his entire body of work (certainly one of the funniest, and therefore among the most Nietzschean) we find the famous relationship between lambs and birds of prey. The lambs, victims of an endless violence, commiserate,

> [...] "these birds of prey are evil; and whoever is least like a bird
> of prey, but rather its opposite, a lamb—would he not be good?"
> [... T]he birds of prey might view it a little ironically and say: "*we*
> don't dislike them at all, these good little lambs; we even love them:
> nothing is more tasty than a tender lamb." (1887/1989b, pp. 44–45)

What is crucial to recognize here is that Nietzsche is not just being ironic; he is describing the way in which empathy and cruelty are not necessarily, intrinsically opposed. This is the essential insight of Nietzsche's ethics. In context, the parable pertains to the historical relationship between the early Christians and their aristocratic Roman persecutors. Delight in the brutal excesses of the coliseum testifies not to some cold, hateful heart on the part of the intoxicated revelers, but just the opposite: a joyful affirmation of the immanent world of hierarchy and power. Christianity, as Nietzsche sees it, will politicize this immanence, in a psychological gesture that inscribes the most devastating historical effects: "You poor Romans, enjoying so much cruelty—how badly you must feel deep down inside yourselves, to find such pleasure in our suffering. And for that, we not only pity you, we forgive you ...".

It is right at this moment that Nietzsche locates the most profound reversal of traditional, Homeric values. When one willfully greets death in the resigned attitude of pity, and grants forgiveness to those who would rejoice in the bloody spectacle of violence, something anti-traditional, anti-historical occurs. An interiority is carved out in the affective discharge of the strong, which begins to function as an obstacle to enjoyment by discrediting the intrinsic nobility of joy. Nietzsche understands that this is a purely affective exchange, prior to and more powerful than language or discourse (1886/1989a, p. 23; p. 35). Faced with the gestures of pity and forgiveness—gestures not merely spoken but enacted, lived out in a pre-discursive, pre-symbolic way—the predator is forced to assume a position in which he has done something that incurs guilt, something not just bad but "evil": "You forgive me? I hadn't realized I'd done something wrong..." This is the sense in which forgiveness constitutes an exercise of domination. It is not just a reversal of values, but a reversal of positions from which value might be evaluated in the first place. If I am forgiven, what is implied is my ignorance as to some ultimate, transcendental law according to which true value ought to be assigned. Empathy and enjoyment are in this way split apart, in a priority assigned to seriousness and to self-sacrifice. The result is what Nietzsche calls "bad conscience." Predation is forced to reflect upon itself, and to judge itself as crime, in a reversal that elevates suffering to the status of universal moral virtue. The effects of this reversal, as Nietzsche sees it, have determined the course of the last 2000 years of Western history.

Infancy, aggression, splitting

Klein offers a theory of boundary formation in primitive mental states. The most basic task the mind faces is to hold itself together without falling to pieces by attempting to simply expel painful tensions whenever they arise. Freud sees the primary function of the mind as regulating the inner experience of self; Klein sees that our inner worlds are stably internal only in relation to an outer world that must be put in its proper place, and that this relationship is perpetually drawn and redistributed at every moment of psychic life. Pathology stems from not being able to take back in what has been externalized, insisting on experiencing what is inside as if it were really outside, aggressively denying the boundary or difference between the two.

Klein begins at the limits of Freud's reflections, in those places Freud initially staked out but from which he respectfully withdrew. In the "Formulations on the two principles of mental functioning" of 1911, Freud offers a highly speculative account of the mind's earliest encounters with the external world. He talks there about the formation of two different egos—two different relationships to experience—a pleasure ego and a reality ego, each dominated by one of the two principles: the pleasure principle (the need to reduce tension) or the reality principle (the need to accommodate environmental demands in order to survive). In this rudimentary organization of mental life, pleasurable experiences are idealized, while unpleasurable experiences are repudiated. On Klein's account, either something is "all good"—and if that is the case, it is identified with the nascent sense of self—or it is "all bad"—in which case it is refused as part of the world. The logic at work here is one of absolute opposition, without gradation, without ambiguity, as the infant attempts to deal with its position of fundamental helplessness.

Freud (1915e) writes that the unconscious recognizes no time, no absence, no negation. Klein extends this insight to develop a picture of the infant's phenomenal experience itself. The center of the infant's world is the breast, upon which its survival absolutely depends. When it is hungry and wants to be fed, the baby does not feel the absence of the "good" breast that feeds it, it experiences the presence of a "bad," enemy breast. Absence is not absence but an attacking, malevolent presence. When what the baby wants is not there, this is experienced as if something unwanted *is* there. The absence of the good is the presence of the bad. Hunger is not experienced as a lack of pleasurable satisfaction, but as a devastating attack on the baby's existence itself. In response to that attack, Klein understands, the baby attempts to get rid of its experience—evacuate it, deny its very reality—split it off. When the hungry baby cries, the cry is not a call, it is an attempt to get rid of the experience of hunger as if it were a bad object. For Klein, the cry of the hungry baby is not the symbolic expression of inner suffering; it is akin to the spontaneous barks and growls of a cornered animal attempting to ward off a threatening predator. Raging at the object, the baby directs its aggression outwards. Of course, since its hunger is internal, the hunger does not go away, but this only reinforces the paranoid onslaught to which the baby feels itself subjected. Its own aggression seems to return to it from the outside, the bad object gets even worse, and the baby's own rage and hatred are redoubled. This is the basic dilemma of early infancy: In very primitive mental states, there is no "I am hungry," since there is yet no sense of "I." There is rather an experience of being threatened by something that takes satisfaction, well-being, safety, *away*—and not "away from *me*," but *radically away* in a terrifying, catastrophic sense.

In order to introduce the concept of projective identification at this point, recall Nietzsche's description of will to power as a pre-subjective differential of force:

> [...] in all willing there is, first, a plurality of sensations, namely, the state *"away from which,"* the sensation of the state *"towards which,"* the sensations of this *"from"* and *"towards"* themselves, and then also an accompanying muscular condensation, which, even without our putting into motion "arms and legs," begins its action by force of habit as soon as we "will" anything.

This primacy of "from" and "towards" describes the phenomenal contours of the psychic mechanisms of projection and introjection. For Klein, the baby is caught up in an abyss of "towards" and "away," splitting its mental experience apart in order to manage primitive existential terror. Nietzsche's revolutionary concept of the will finds its correlate here in Klein's understanding of unconscious phantasy, as a kind of thinking that is pre-linguistic, pre-discursive, pre-representational—a "thinking" that is not "about" anything, but that is continuous with bodily action. With the concept of will to power, Nietzsche attempts to work out this very same level of pre-subjective ("unphilosophical") experience.

Like Nietzsche, Klein bases her project on the presence of an inherent capacity to evaluate experience in terms of good and bad. She casts Freud's pleasure and reality principles in terms of an effort at evaluative judgment under the sway of an aggressive drive that seeks to express itself in the affective form of power and command. For Klein, more so than for Freud, the infant does not just want to avoid reality, but to force reality to conform to the demands of unconscious phantasy. What Klein offers is a meticulous account of the dynamics of pre-subjective relations that Nietzsche had charged philosophy with having not only ignored but having constitutively repressed—or, better, split off.

Furthermore, Nietzsche's assessment of pity anticipates Klein's understanding of the role of envy in early mental life. For Freud, if we want to understand the experience of mind, we have to understand the centrality of anxiety; for Klein, what is more basic to our constitution is envy. The Kleinian distinction between envy and jealously asserts that in jealousy, I wish I had what the other has—what the other has is exciting to me, I wish I were in the other's place. Envy is essentially more destructive: When I envy the other, I don't just wish I had the good thing she has, I want to spoil and destroy the thing's very goodness in order to deprive the other of an experience that I myself am deprived of, to make us the same. In drawing the distinction between envy and jealousy, Klein (1975/2002) writes:

> Envy is the angry feeling that another person possesses and enjoys something desirable—the envious impulse being to take it away or to spoil it. Moreover, envy implies the subject's relation to one person only and goes back to the earliest exclusive relation with the mother. Jealousy is based on envy, but involves a relation to at least two people; it is mainly concerned with love that the subject feels is his due and has been taken away, or is in danger of being taken away, from him by his rival. In the everyday conception of jealousy, a man or woman feels deprived of the loved person by somebody else. (p. 181)

Jealousy observes difference: I wish I had what you have—I wish I were you. Envy denies difference: If I can't have what you have, you can't have it either—both of us should suffer. At its extreme, envy constitutes an attack on the very being of the other: I don't just want to enjoy what you enjoy, I want you never to have existed as enjoying it in the first place. Envy is in this sense an attack not just on the object, but on time and difference as such. Nietzsche had conceived pity similarly as based in an effort to abolish the other's capacity for enjoyment: The lamb has recourse only to pity and forgiveness when faced with an other that celebrates its demise. Incapable of any physical display of strength, "weakness" here consists in a psychological projection of resentment and hatred that is effectively capable of disrupting the active pleasures of empathy and predation.

Nowhere does the psychoanalytic literature more closely approximate Nietzsche's description of the subject of metaphysics than in Klein's account of the infant's relation to the breast where this relation is dominated by primitive sadism and envy: "Envy contributes to the infant's difficulties in building up his good object, for he feels that the gratification of which he was deprived has been kept for itself by the breast that frustrated him" (Klein, 1975/2002, p. 180). The baby is on this account subject to each of the "four errors" that Nietzsche outlines as forming the basis of the metaphysical outlook:

1. The error of confusing cause and effect: that the breast causes hunger, rather than hunger causing the interpretation of the breast as "bad."
2. The error of false causation: that the "bad" breast enforces hunger, rather than hunger being a condition of bodily need.
3. The error of imaginary causes: splitting apart and idealization of the "bad" and "good" breasts as the origins of pain and pleasure.
4. The error of free will: that projecting envy and rage constitutes a relation by means of which a subject can manipulate an object.

Each of these positions is formulated as a vengeful, "teeth-gnashing" response to temporality and to the gap between need and satisfaction. The Kleinian infant is a reactive, oppositional, time-hating metaphysician.

On Klein's account, it is not necessary that the infant suffer actual environmental deprivation; rather it can, because of such a "weak constitution," suffer from an intrinsic inability to forget the prior absence or delay of satisfaction even after its needs have been met. "If envy is excessive," Klein (1975/2002) writes, "this, in my view, indicates that paranoid and schizoid features are abnormally strong and that such an infant can be regarded as ill" (p. 183). The extent to which Nietzsche's and Klein's analyses converge on this point make it tempting to derive the weakness of "slave morality" from the paranoid-schizoid position. For Nietzsche, pity and forgiveness attempt to spoil the intrinsic goodness of the other's experience of autonomy: If I can't have what you have, you can't either, everything must be the same. Envious and incapable of enjoying power, slave morality intends to ruin the goodness of power as such. In Kleinian terms, this describes the baby's aggressive relation to the mother who controls access to the omnipotent goodness that it is convinced the breast *is*. With the *Genealogy of Morals*, Nietzsche had already written the Kleinian infant's experience large in offering up the underlying logic of the history of institutional Christianity.

In her seminal 1946 paper "Notes on some schizoid mechanisms," Klein writes that in early mental life, where again, frustration mobilizes an aggressive hatred of reality as against those parts of the self that contain or are identified with the phenomenal experience of frustration,

> Much of the hatred against parts of the self is directed [...] against the mother. This leads to a particular form of identification which establishes the prototype of an aggressive [relationship]. I suggest for these processes the term "projective identification." When projection is mainly derived from the infant's impulse to harm or to control the mother, he feels her to be a persecutor. In psychotic disorders this identification of the object with the hated parts of the self contributes to an intensity of the hatred directed against other people. As far as the ego is concerned the excessive splitting off and expelling into the outer world of part of itself considerably weakens it. For the aggressive component of feelings and of the personality is intimately bound up in the mind with power, potency, strength, knowledge and many other desired qualities. (1986, p. 183)

Projective identification appeared here in passing, without indication of the central place it would assume in her thinking and for her followers. As the prototype of an aggressive relationship, it describes the way in which suffering can be evacuated, first by splitting off those parts of the self that feel or that "contain" suffering, inserting these "bad" parts of self into the experience of the other (causing the other person to suffer in my place)—this is the projective aspect. Once the tormented parts of the self are put inside the mind and body of someone else, the difference between self and other is erased so that the "bad" parts can be controlled and kept at a safe distance—this is the identification. What this means is that I put those aspects of my experience that I can't tolerate into you, as aspects of your experience, not mine, and making you miserable in this way from then on constitutes the basis of our ongoing relationship. As fantastic as this sounds, it describes an everyday clinical event: The patient cannot tolerate aspects of his reality that the analysis inevitably happens upon. Rather than own those experiences or "parts of self" that had previously been split off and denied, they are projected into the analyst, who now appears not as someone who led the patient to aspects of himself that he would rather not accept, but as the living embodiment of those bad parts—a real, external persecutor.

The historical complexity of the relationship is reduced to an eternally present antagonism (Ogden, 1986, p. 62). For Klein, meaning is generated in the dynamic interplay of introjection and projection. Projective identification collapses this interplay into a fixed, self-evident opposition.

In conceiving projective identification in this way—as a both an *intra*-psychic and an *inter*-psychic procedure—Klein brings psychoanalysis closer to Nietzsche than Freud ever did. What she describes is how, the more we exercise our aggression in a primitive manner by means of projective identification, the weaker self-experience becomes. The angrier one gets, the less *actual* power one is capable of demonstrating, because overwhelming envy and hatred are driven to demarcate the boundary between self and world in terms of the absolute otherness of the "all bad." The more hateful one is, the more fragile and insufficient is one's ability to deal with that hatred. Klein thinks this downward spiral in terms of a weakening of the possibility of autonomy. Nietzsche had described this same movement (despite his critique of all logics of opposition) in terms of an opposition between the "weak" and the "strong." Klein offers a more meticulous analysis, according to which one can witness how the "weak" personality—the one who hates, envies, covets, resents—*becomes* weak, by giving up on an inherent strength capable of power and differentiation, succumbing instead to a tendency toward destructiveness that enforces a homogeneity of self and world.

In a late paper on "Our adult world and its roots in infancy," Klein writes:

> By projecting oneself or part of one's impulses and feelings into another person, an identification with that person is achieved [...] On the other hand, putting part of oneself into the other person (projecting), the identification is based on attributing to the other person some of one's own qualities [...]. We are inclined to attribute to other people—in a sense, to put into them—some of our own emotions and thoughts; and it is obvious that it will depend on how balanced or persecuted we are whether this projection is of a friendly or a hostile nature. By attributing part of our feelings to the other person, we understand their feelings, needs, and satisfactions; in other words, we are putting ourselves into the other person's shoes. There are people who go so far in this direction that they lose themselves entirely in others and become incapable of objective judgement. (Quoted in Britton, 1998, p. 5)

Two points are worth noting with regard to this passage:

First, it is clear that what is at issue is not any attempt to negotiate some irreducible opposition between psychic and material reality, "inside" and "outside." Such an opposition can be assigned no intrinsic primacy in human life. Rather, introjection and projection describe self-identity as an ongoing, dynamic process of development. "Taking things in" and "putting them out" are unconscious phantasies about this process itself.

Second, this is also clearly an attempt at understanding the psychological origins of empathy as an effort at "putting oneself in the other's place." In this passage projective identification is not conceived as inherently aggressive or pathological; it is at the same time what makes possible mutual respect and understanding. If our impulses lean more in the direction of hatred rather than love, however, what would otherwise be felt as empathy forms the basis for experiences of the most frightening persecution. When she writes, "There are people who go so far in this direction that they lose themselves entirely in others and become incapable of objective judgement," Klein indicates that certain psychotics have not abandoned all contact with the reality of other people; rather they are so open to, empathize with others so painfully, so voraciously, that as a result their basic sense of self feels constantly under threat of total annihilation.

Writing from a contemporary Kleinian perspective, Ronald Britton (1998) links this latter experience to what the poet Rilke evocatively described in his *Duino Elegies*, where, "whenever he [Rilke] was prompted to love or felt loved, he felt he risked losing his identity" (p. 5). It is not difficult to appreciate how this could describe both the origins of severe forms of psychopathology, and the essence of any possible ethical position. In order to tease out the distinction, without laying claim to its ever being perfectly clear, Britton distinguishes two faces of projective identification. The first is one in which "*I am you.*" This is projective identification as it forms the basis of empathic attunement: I "take you in," in such a way that I can genuinely feel your experience within myself. As Nietzsche indicates at the end of Book Two of *Daybreak* (1881/1997b, pp. 146–148), sickness can emerge from an overinvestment in such a capacity. In other words, at its origin, the very possibility of an ethical judgment is rooted in an irreducible openness to the experience of psychosis. You have to be at least a little bit crazy to care about anything, and the more you care, the crazier it can feel.

A second, more disturbed form of projective identification is expressed in Britton's figure, "*You are me.*" In this case, an aspect or "part" of the self is attributed to the other, and in such a way that generates in the other a compulsion to behave in the manner of those split off and projected parts. This is what the concept of projective identification more familiarly describes in the Kleinian literature. What I find unacceptable in me, I put into you, in a way that forces you to experience it, and to feel and behave accordingly, so that I don't have to.

On the one hand, then: "*I am you*"—*l'effet c'est moi.* In making oneself thoroughly available to the world—and this again is what "strength" means, for Nietzsche—the experience of being a self emerges as the effect of an engagement with (rather than a refusal of) otherness, manifested in the world as hierarchy, differentiation, and command. This marks the way our conscious sense of self or self-identity does not originally or causally direct action, but rather emerges as the after-effect of an unconscious affirmation of active engagements in fields of power, difference, and enjoyment.

On the other hand: "*You are me*"—*l'effet c'est toi.* On this condition, the other emerges only as a narcissistic extension of myself, and for the both of us: I experience you as the embodiment of my own paranoid, subjective fantasies, and you feel compelled to act as if these were literally, objectively true. Nietzsche had already diagnosed this non-metaphysical, pre-subjective exchange in the coercive power of ascetic monotheism: "You poor beast of prey, I understand you better than you seem to understand yourself, and after all, isn't that shameful?" This is not properly a question, it is an assertion of force that forecloses thoughtfulness and that compels agreement and conformity.

The cruelty of the frame

In his commentary on Nietzsche's critique of *ressentiment*, Deleuze (1962/1983) asks, "What is the mechanism of this 'sickness'?" (p. 111). The "sickness" of *ressentiment* (which insists, "it's all your fault") rests on the becoming-reactive of will to power, such that the will is not something acted on but internalized and suffered from. For Nietzsche, this reactive turning inward organizes cognitive processes, inaugurating a sense of "irreducible subjectivity" (Renik, 1993). As a result, the resentful type *knows* (in an affective, "unphilosophical" way) that the other is evil, and that he, in turn, is the embodiment of the good. As Deleuze makes clear, however, *ressentiment* should not be understood simply as a feeling, but as a "mechanical," twofold process: "The process of accusation in *ressentiment* fulfills this task: Reactive forces 'project' an abstract and neutralized image of force" (p. 123). This projection is secondary with respect to a prior splitting: "Moment of causality: force is split in two [...]. An imaginary relation of causality is substituted for a real relation of significance. Force is first repressed into itself, then its manifestation is made into a different thing which finds its distinct, efficient cause in the force" (ibid.). First then, the splitting of activity and its effect, by means of which an underlying cause or subject is deduced; second, a projective attribution of malevolent "evil" to this other, which remains naive or "abstract" as a merely inverted mirror image of the "good" sense of self that has triumphantly emerged. Thus, as Deleuze writes, "*Ressentiment* [...] has two aspects or moments [...] *reversal* of the relation of forces, *projection* of a reactive image [...]" (p. 124; emphases in original).

Klein had discerned this very same gesture, although she had described it in the opposite direction: First the projection of intolerable aspects of self, then the denial of any difference between self and other, by means of which the other is reduced to being a satellite of the fragmented and destructive, attacking self-organization. Clearly familiar with, yet unwilling fully to assume the Kleinian terminology, Deleuze writes, "In *ressentiment* reactive force accuses and projects itself. But *ressentiment* would be nothing if it did not lead the accused himself to admit his wrongs, to 'turn back to himself': The *introjection* of reactive force is not the opposite of *projection* but the consequence and continuation of reactive projection" (p. 128; emphases in original). Projective identification—what Deleuze here calls, in terms indebted to both Klein and Nietzsche, "reactive projection"—describes a continuous denial of any difference that would allow for a distinction between self and other, past and present, strength and weakness to emerge in the first place.

Clinical example

A relatively high functioning patient (L) initially sought help because of his chronic lateness, which had begun to alienate him from his friends and was threatening to get him fired from his job. No matter how hard he tried, L just couldn't show up for anything on time. Some months into our work together, the symptom was all but gone. He was showing up to everything on time—work, social engagements, etc.—everything except, of course, the analysis. Many years later, L is still consistently about five minutes late, and he always blames this on the unreliability of the city subway trains. Together we have explored this from several different angles: When L is late, he fantasizes that I think he must be doing something terribly exciting, that he is a busy, important person. At the same time, he imagines that I get anxious, something must have happened to him and I'm left worrying that he is hurt. In addition, if he were to show up even a minute early, sitting in my waiting room would make him furious, because if our connection were "truly real," he says, I wouldn't make him wait to see me. These are all completely accurate interpretations, but none of them makes any difference. Day after day L is late and I have to contain my annoyance and not lash out at him, which is clearly what he is trying to provoke me into doing. On top of it all, L complains that our four hours per week together are not enough, that he wishes he could see me for several hours each and every day.

One Thursday, L announces that although he had forgotten to mention it previously, he had booked a flight out of town for the next day and would not be able to make our appointment—could we reschedule for earlier in the morning? I told him I was unable to do so at such a late hour, but he would still be responsible for paying for the session, and I wondered why he hadn't asked sooner. Irritated, L said he had simply "put it out of mind." On further questioning he said that the fact that I wasn't willing to reschedule was evidence that I didn't really care about him. After all, there had been instances in the past when I had to cancel at a moment's notice, wasn't it only fair that he should be allowed to do the same? As the anger and resentment in his voice became increasingly palpable, he said this was evidence that our relationship was "just business." If that weren't the case, he insisted, if I *really* cared about him, why would I charge him? Why was I so "cruel"? Didn't I *know* how bad the economy is? Didn't I *know* after all this time about his credit card debt? And yet I *make* him keep coming to see me day after day for such an outrageous amount of money!

Aware that agency (who is doing what to whom) is something L struggles with, I say, "When you go away, it feels like I'm leaving you."

The next session after the long weekend, L shows up two minutes early. He opens by saying that last night he'd had a vivid, disturbing dream. In the dream, he is at a lovely, serene summer cottage. He is standing on a dock that overlooks a pond below. In the pond, he sees a turtle. The turtle is tiny but, he says, "its geometry is exquisite." Suddenly the pond is teeming with thousands of turtles. Then he notices a log, which transforms into a large anaconda snake. Then there are several anacondas, and the pond is not a pond but a pit, with no water, just organisms writhing all over one another. The pit is full of life, he says, but there is no food to sustain it. Looking down, at first he feels scared, then he feels extremely lonely, thinking, "Nobody will ever know what this looks like ..." When he is done telling the dream, L asks me if I've ever been to the Florida Everglades.

As I listen to the material, I imagine that the turtles are minutely fragmented, psychotic parts of L himself, teeming inside but split apart, unaware of one another. The snakes articulate his aggression, which causes him to be impulsive and to ruin relationships (like with being late). His mind is a writhing, starving, suffocating pit, and as much as this terrifies him, it is also a state he idealizes (it's "exquisite"). Of course, I don't say any of this. What I do comment on is his fear and loneliness in the dream, linking this to his question about me, if I've seen the Everglades—if I could ever truly know what goes on inside him. He says that although he had been away, he had felt close to me over the weekend because of our last session. And yet, that closeness is also the source of an immense sadness.

From a Kleinian perspective, what is essential is that L experiences me as withholding: I have all the good stuff, but I obstinately refuse to just give it to him; he should not have to ask me for what he wants, and when he does, I should acquiesce without delay. This is the omnipotent power the infant attributes to the breast, pitying itself for its absolute, unjust deprivation. Waiting until the last minute to tell me about his impending absence, L tries to get me to feel his sense of total abandonment, so that he can manipulatively dump all of his badness into me and leave it behind, allowing him to enjoy the weekend away. I gently indicate my understanding that he is attacking our connectedness, and I can tolerate that—I'll still be there for him when he gets back. This helps L maintain our connection by short-circuiting the projective identification. When he returns, he feels guilty about his anger. His sense of autonomy is enhanced, but this involves a mourning of our essential separation and difference, which he otherwise tries so desperately and in so many ways to avoid having to acknowledge.

What might Nietzsche say about all this? It sounds like we are far from anything Nietzsche is concerned with, but we are not, we are right at the heart of Nietzsche's ethics. L's "guilt" is not guilt in an ordinary sense, because my acceptance of his aggression is not a gesture of forgiveness. His sadness indicates that he is actually in a much better place than he had been in before leaving. My interpretation forces him to encounter the power differential that divides us, but in a way that puts him in an exalted position (looking *down* at the pit, rather than being just another hungry, lost, little turtle). He feels "bad," but he feels *alive*—connected—and this is vastly different from the badness he felt when he secretly booked his flight away. His sadness, for once, is not a sign of manic hopelessness but of gratitude. By refusing to rearrange my schedule on a moment's notice, I had met L in the affect of command. Rather than feel subordinated, he responded in kind with will to power by remaining actively engaged with me while he was away, instead of reactively devaluing our differences and forgetting ("putting out of mind") our connectedness. Instead of being "supportive," in the way we typically think about what that means, I had remained committed to our arrangement by affirming its intrinsic hierarchy. What facilitated the shift toward psychic integration was my ability to maintain resolutely ("cruelly," in L's experience) the neutrality of the analytic frame. This issued from a shared commitment to the interpretive, differential power relationship (the transference) that L and I had agreed to work through together. Such a commitment is precisely what Nietzsche had advocated, as against the degenerative tide of pity, weakness, and fundamentalism.

Strength

In addition to its usual connotations, projective identification can be understood as a compulsive finding of fault in the world, where the world has been reduced to nothing more than an empty container of undesirable parts of oneself; it describes the degradation of human relationships by means of a defensive, global ruining that collapses the space of meaningful, symbolic interaction. For Nietzsche, the priest, as the prototype of all authoritarian figures, is the institutional embodiment of this trajectory. Condemning the healthy and the strong, the priest says: "You make *us* suffer because *you* feel bad." Inhibiting will to power in this way establishes an interiority replete with the ecstatic pain of self-hatred and guilt. This is why *ressentiment* resists interpretation classically conceived (as indistinct from explanation), why it cannot be argued with, in that it serves as its own source of narcissistic reward.

You cannot convince someone that it feels good not to feel bad when feeling bad feels so good. This resentful, narcissistic self-satisfaction is precisely what slave morality calls for as an absence of all conflict and an idealized fantasy of equality that both Klein and Nietzsche recognize as a desire for stasis and death:

> The absence of conflict in the infant, if such a hypothetical state could be imagined, would deprive him of enrichment of his personality and of an important factor in the strengthening of his ego. For conflict, and the need to overcome it, is a fundamental element in creativeness. (Klein, 2002, p. 186)

Here Klein most clearly expresses, if not a direct indebtedness to Nietzsche, then at the very least her indebtedness to a general intellectual culture for which Nietzsche was a central figure and inspiration. The absence of conflict is detrimental to the development of creativity; it deprives the individual of conditions of strife and struggle by means of which individuality as a creative condition is won in the first place. Like the infant raging against indications that its perceived omnipotence is only a fantasy, an impossibly conflict-free state—eternal and beyond the constraints of human finitude—is precisely what metaphysics, in its religious, political, and psychological forms, falsely promises.

Klein's thinking is in this way more fully capable of tracing the movement Nietzsche portrays from *ressentiment* in the weak to bad conscience and nihilism in the strong: from "it's all your fault!" to "it's all my fault," to "who cares anyway ..." Projective identification might be thought not so much as an attack on the other as object, but as an attack on will to power as active, individuating process. Insisting on logics of rigid opposition, projective identification spreads negativity and sameness, resulting in hopelessness, helplessness, and nihilism. If nihilism expresses a pervasive tendency toward bad conscience, apathy, and disinterest—as away from empathy, excitement, and care—this is because nihilism constitutes a refusal to encounter what in and of itself means nothing, but that first makes meaning possible, and so must be affirmed: what Nietzsche had otherwise called, simply, life.

CHAPTER FOUR

Nietzsche, Winnicott, play

A man's maturity—consists in having found again the seriousness
one had as a child, at play.

—Nietzsche, *Beyond Good and Evil*

A t the end of *The Gay Science* (*Book Five*: "We fearless ones"),
Nietzsche addresses, "We who are new, nameless, hard to
understand; we premature births of an as yet unproved future,"
in whose name he calls "for a new end, we also need a new means,
namely, a new health that is stronger, craftier, tougher, bolder, and more
cheerful than any previous health" (1882/2001, p. 246). What Nietzsche
generally means by "strength" is contained in this passage. He speaks
of, "*the great health*, a health that one doesn't only have, but also acquires
continually and must acquire because one gives it up again and again,
and must give it up!" For those who have provisionally acceded to such
health, Nietzsche asks, "how could we still be satisfied with *modern-day
man*?" Modern-day man conceives health as the successful avoidance
of illness. Nietzsche will see this as a reactive condition that embraces
mediocrity. His concept of health as strength is one that requires an
effort to think illness not as health's opposite but as a necessary passage

through which we must repeatedly return in order to remain healthy—that is, powerful. In psychoanalytic terms: The strength of the ego can be measured by its capacity for controlled regression within the clinical setting.

At stake for Nietzsche here, as always, is the question of the relationship to ideals—to the future. The commonsense ideals of "modern-day man" are the ideals of metaphysics: certainty, knowledge, and stability, by means of which the future might be strategically anticipated and controlled. Adherence to such ideals is measured in terms of the lowest and most vulgar forms today, most often via competition reduced to demonstrations of exploitative phallic prowess. These are ideals that Nietzsche will associate with nihilism, slave morality, and herd mentality—the "intentional stupidity" of "commercial culture." In contrast, Nietzsche offers a conception of health defined by its ability to embrace risk, uncertainty, and chance:

> Another ideal runs before us, a peculiar, seductive, *dangerous ideal* to which we wouldn't want to persuade anyone, since we don't readily concede the right to it to anyone: *the ideal of a spirit that plays naively*, i.e. not deliberately but from overflowing abundance and power, with everything that was hitherto called holy, good, untouchable, divine; a spirit which has gone so far that the highest thing which the common people quite understandably accepts as its measure of value would signify for it danger, decay, debasement, or at any rate recreation, blindness, temporary self-oblivion: the ideal of a human, superhuman well-being and benevolence that will often enough appear *inhuman*—for example, when it places itself next to all earthly seriousness heretofore, all forms of solemnity in gesture, word, tone, look, morality, and task as if it were their most incarnate and involuntary parody—and in spite of all this, it is perhaps only with it that *the great seriousness* really emerges; that the real question mark is posed for the first time; that the destiny of the soul changes; the hand of the clock moves forward; the tragedy begins. (1882/2001, p. 247; emphases modified)

The originality of Nietzsche's effort here might not be immediately apparent. It is to have dissociated the notion of what is *ideal* from what is *right*. To say that something is ideal is to indicate that it is inherently good. To move from a concept of the ideal to that of right is to universalize what is irreducibly particular—to assert that *my* good is good for *all*. For Nietzsche, the European Enlightenment discourse concerning "human rights" is itself a means of exerting power and authority by universalizing individual ideals. Nietzsche's "dangerous ideal" is dangerous to the extent that it resists universalization, proclaiming a "good" that is not necessarily good for all. This is because health is not a singular condition that everyone shares. What might promote the life of one might be poison for another.

How then is it possible to speak any longer of ideals in this sense? Ideals are by definition extratemporal, and as such they are the province of metaphysics. One would expect Nietzsche as anti-metaphysician to have abandoned all talk about ideals. If it seems odd that he continues to speak—insistently, even—about ideals, this is a measure of how difficult his thinking has proven to assimilate. The "dangerous ideal" of which Nietzsche writes is "peculiar, seductive." Its unique seductive power lies in the fact that it is not universal, therefore not "good" in the traditional sense—a "dangerous ideal" that is at once a "dangerous 'maybe'" (1886/1989a, p. 11). What Nietzsche indicates by the "inhuman" is not the "immoral" in the sense of the sadistic, but what cannot be contained within any concept of humanity as universal (rational, moral) subject. What is inhuman, for Nietzsche, is immoral in the sense that it refuses any definition of the human as that which subordinates itself to universal categories or expectations. What is human can be "good" only to the extent that it pursues ideals that are not intended to offer themselves up democratically as general principles for everybody. The more the good and the ideal coincide to form a concept of general "health," the more conditions of weakness prevail under pretenses that claim a right to call themselves commonsense, culture, or reality.

Against Platonic-Christian moral ideals Nietzsche counterposes, "the ideal of a spirit that plays naively, i.e. not deliberately but from overflowing abundance and power ..." Nietzsche's sense of playfulness is joyful but not at all frivolous, consistently linked to what he calls "seriousness," which is to be distinguished from solemnity and lack of humor. Among the aphorisms collected in Part Four of *Beyond Good and Evil*, Nietzsche writes, "A man's maturity—consists in having found again the seriousness one had as a child, at play" (1886/1989a, p. 83). Play is process-oriented, not goal-oriented; it requires a safe, continuous environment, a regular and clearly demarcated space and time set apart from ordinary reality. Huizinga (1938/1971) described this as a "magic circle"—a separate reality that establishes an active stance, a sense of initiative issuing onto creative freedom. For Nietzsche, to be able to appreciate the seriousness of play, and to determine what play has to teach us, requires a particular kind of scientific rigor. Play is something that scientific positivism cannot think. In Nietzsche's terms this reflects the triumph of reactive forces in the interpretation of nature according to a classical framework that opposes immanence and transcendence, truth and untruth, subjectivity and objectivity. A "maturity" both of self and of science demands an alternative to this framework. This chapter will argue that psychoanalysis offers just such an alternative, and that to appreciate Nietzsche's understanding of the seriousness of play is to encounter what it means to work with a genuinely dynamic unconscious.

Play, power, becoming

According to Lawrence Hinman (1974), if there is any concept that ties together the entirety of Nietzsche's work into a form that begins to approach systematicity, it is that of play. Hinman opposes those readers like Heidegger who would impose on Nietzsche's thinking a systematic form to which the concepts of will to power and eternal recurrence can be assigned a centrally organizing role, but he concedes that the concept of play might well be considered to function in this way. In this he follows Heidegger's student Eugen Fink, who wrote, "where Nietzsche grasps being and becoming as *Spiel*, he no longer stands in the confinement of metaphysics" (quoted in Shrift, 1990, p. 63). Play is the exit from metaphysical thinking, both in theory and in practice.

As Tracy Strong (1975) indicates, the German word *spielen* has a different inflection than the English "playing" (p. 278). In addition to referring to the activity we typically associate with children, it also implicates the sense of "play" as game and risk. It is both innocent and dangerous, "serious" in the sense that one can lose oneself in playing like the child for hours on end, but one always and inherently risks losing oneself in a more devastating and irreversible way, as with the adult ruined financially and emotionally by gambling. *Spielen* implicates laughter and joyful abandon, but also the absence of foundation, affirming the compulsion to pursue an abyss common to both creativity and addiction.

Nietzsche's preoccupation with play dates to his earliest writings, particularly those in which he discusses the Pre-Socratic Greeks. Among the ancients, the one Nietzsche most identified with was Heraclitus. In

Heraclitus, Nietzsche finds the first great champion of becoming over and against Being—the affirmation of finite time over delusions of eternity. Heraclitus is most famous for his statement, "It is not possible to step into the same river twice." He denied the existence of anything that endures without succumbing to transformation and change, identifying the primary elemental force in the natural world as fire. This was such a bizarre and counterintuitive thought that Heraclitus was known to his ancient contemporaries as "The Obscure" and "The Riddler" (Curd, 2011, p. 39). Two fragments, both reported by Hippolytus in his *Refutation of All Heresies*, are particularly relevant to understanding Nietzsche's attraction:

> War is the father of all and king of all, and some he shows as gods, others as humans; some he makes slaves, others free. (ibid., p. 47)

> A lifetime is a child playing, playing checkers; the kingdom belongs to a child. (ibid., p. 52)

In the first fragment, the Greek for "war" can also be translated as "conflict" or "strife"; "father" might be translated as "origin." In the second fragment, "lifetime" can also be translated as "eternity," and "kingdom" as "kingship." Where "origin" is "conflict," what is implied is the absence of any origin as singular, reliable ground: Conflict implies difference, multiplicity, uncertainty. "War is the father of all and king of all" is a profoundly paradoxical statement that invokes the power of fathers and kings in order to denounce the authority of fathers, kings, and power. With Heraclitus, as against the Aristotelian identification of cognition with logic, paradox is the essence of active thinking:

> Heraclitus' regal possession is his extraordinary power to think intuitively. Toward the other type of thinking, the type that is accomplished in concepts and logical combinations, in other words towards reason, he shows himself cool, insensitive, in fact hostile, and seems to feel pleasure whenever he can contradict it with an intuitively arrived-at truth. He does this in dicta like "Everything forever has its opposite along with it," and in such unabashed fashion that Aristotle accused him of the highest crime before the tribunal of reason: to have sinned against the law of contradiction. (Nietzsche, 1962, p. 52)

It is tempting to claim that Heraclitus is the first to have acknowledged what Freud would call "primary process" thinking, but there is more at stake here than the mere absence of time and negation. In striking the concept of Being from his ontology, Heraclitus affirms strife and play as the conditions of thinking in a way that erases the opposition between them. The unity of strife and play articulates becoming as a theory of time that Nietzsche finds inescapably challenging and intoxicating:

> He [Heraclitus] repeatedly says of it [time] that every moment in
> it exists only insofar as it has just consumed the preceding one, its
> father, and is then immediately consumed likewise. And that past
> and future are as perishable as any dream, but that the present is
> but the dimensionless and durationless borderline between the
> two. And that space is just like time, and that everything which
> coexists in space and time has but a relative existence through and
> for another like it, which is to say through and for an equally rel-
> evant one. (ibid., p. 53)

Heraclitean becoming, in which space and time are revealed as "dimensionless and durationless borderline[s]"—as differentiating-difference—is what Nietzsche will call "will to power." It is in Heraclitean becoming as play—the vision of which cannot be deduced from logic, which "cannot be guessed by dialectic detective work nor figured out with the help of calculations" (ibid., p. 58)—that Nietzsche discerns the overcoming of the metaphysical the spirit of revenge, of "the will's teeth-gnashing and most lonely affliction" (1884/1961, p. 161), as of "the will's antipathy towards time and time's 'It was'" (p. 162). While Nietzsche will associate this with laughter, he recognizes that the ability to do so does not come naturally—it requires a strenuous effort at self-overcoming:

> The everlasting and exclusive coming-to-be, the impermanence
> of everything actual, which constantly acts and comes-to-be but
> never is, as Heraclitus teaches it, it a terrible, paralyzing thought.
> Its impact on men can most nearly be likened to the sensation dur-
> ing an earthquake when one loses one's familiar confidence in a
> firmly grounded earth. It takes astonishing strength to transform
> this reaction into its opposite, into sublimity and the feeling of
> blessed astonishment. (1962, p. 54)

Implicit in this early passage is Nietzsche's entire critique of metaphysics and the attempt—already realized at the beginning of the philosophical tradition by Heraclitus, in a way that was eclipsed by Plato and buried by Christianity—at challenging metaphysical thinking by affirming becoming as the innocent play of the world. Where becoming or play functions as the central category of ontology—displacing the privilege of atemporal, substantial Being—metaphysics as the attempt at an impossible reversal of time, generative of bad conscience, nihilism, and *ressentiment*, is overcome in a gesture that inaugurates new opportunities for action and new horizons for life. From where does Nietzsche derive his conception of this new form of life? He writes:

> In this world only play, play as artists and children engage in it, exhibits coming-to-be and passing away, structuring and destroying, without any moral additive, in forever equal innocence. And as children and artists play, so plays the ever-living fire. It constructs and destroys, in all innocence. Such is the game that the aeon plays with itself. (ibid., p. 62)

For Nietzsche, especially in the early phase of his work, the child and the artist serve as basic models for conceiving the pursuit of ideals without ideality, for a future that has not been absolutely determined and programmed in advance by a subject who imagines himself capable of deciding "what he wants to be," as if this could be determined in advance of actual, lived experience. Eternal, unchanging ideals are the orientation of the slave's version of power. The child and the artist do not submit themselves to the play of becoming knowing *what* they are going to create, only *that* they are going to create. This is the "innocence" that Nietzsche admired so much, and that he aspired to as the ultimate affirmation of life as will to power. While it is perhaps true that Nietzsche wound up hypostatizing this gesture and repeating the enclosure of metaphysical thinking with the concept of the "Overman," it should be noted that in his *Zarathustra* the symbol that Nietzsche uses to express what elevates itself—what overcomes—in the Overman, over and above the figure of the Lion (the infamous "blond beast"), is that of the Child:

> But tell me, my brothers, what can the child do that even the lion cannot? Why must the preying lion still become a child?

> The child is innocence and forgetfulness, a new beginning, a sport, a self-propelling wheel, a first motion, a sacred Yes.
>
> Yes, a sacred Yes is needed, my brothers, for the sport of creation: The spirit now wills *its own* will, the spirit sundered from the world now wins *its own* world. (1884/1961, p. 55)

Despite the poetic reverie of Nietzsche's *Zarathustra*, we should not fail to appreciate its conceptual rigor. When Nietzsche positions the figure of the child at the apex of the process of self-overcoming, he is not promoting a new figure of the self as having superseded those prior to it. If anything, to project the child as future is to obliterate all forms of historical determinism: to envision the past as future, which is to say to embrace tradition—and not liberation—as the essence of creativity. The Overman as child is not intended to explain human life in terms of some ultimate goal, either of history or of the individual, but on the contrary to indicate that such processes have no goal, are properly liberated or affirmed to the extent that they are recognized—joyfully—as open and indeterminate. The identification of self and becoming that erases the opposition between self and action is what Nietzsche means by "life." Life is not something "I have" ("my life") in contradistinction to a self figured as underlying cause or enduring ground. Nietzsche's theme of play is in this way connected to his critique of causality as a logic belonging to metaphysics. Where cause and effect are expropriated from and opposed to one another in the same manner as subject and object or self and world, historical time can only appear as a source of unjust pain, loss, and *ressentiment*. Nietzsche is constantly at pains to demonstrate that the experience of time as becoming is not an experience "of" time in the sense that one experiences anything else in the form of an object, but experience itself *as* what "constantly acts and comes-to-be but never is ..."

The Heraclitean child perpetually acts but never merely is, existing as process without substantial Being as underlying support. This is an impossible, allegorical child existing without self-consciousness yet capable of exercising a tremendous directive influence on its environment. In Chapter Two, I cited Winnicott's reference to the poet Tagore: "On the seashore of endless worlds, children play." Tagore's line is directly appropriated from Heraclitus, who was said not only to have described existence as a child playing checkers but as a child building sandcastles on a shore, eagerly awaiting the next wave to wash away his creation so as to begin creating again. Both Nietzsche and

Winnicott find inspiration in the Heraclitean intuition of becoming as what cannot be regulated by logical categories. As Nietzsche had been the first to elaborate a philosophical concept of play since Heraclitus—one that destabilized the identification of philosophy with conceptual, logical thought—Winnicott was the first to approach play from a perspective that regards psychoanalysis as something other than science classically conceived (i.e., as dominated by and dominating in the name of logic and the law of non-contradiction). Winnicott embraced his institutional independence as a clinician by foregrounding the concept of "playing," which had been preliminarily elaborated by previous thinkers but had yet to find its specific psychoanalytic voice: "There is something about playing," Winnicott (1971) wrote, "that has not yet found a place in the psychoanalytic literature" (p. 41). Winnicott's work is as notable in the history of psychoanalysis as Nietzsche's work is in the history of philosophy for having refused to submit to logical, commonsense paradigms and for having attended instead to everyday human experience in all its contradictions and strife. Where Nietzsche tended to this domain as that which was retreating and being excluded from everyday life, Winnicott saw the clinic as a domain in which an experience of life as play could be taken up, elaborated upon, and renewed.

Being, doing, playing

Melanie Klein introduced the play technique into psychoanalytic practice in the 1920s, extending and transforming psychoanalytic theory in the process. Klein had insisted that a legitimately Freudian treatment was possible with very young children. Recognizing that children's play functions similarly to free association in analysis with adults, Klein viewed play as the child's natural effort at symbolizing unconscious phantasy. In child analysis one tries to understand and to interpret the child's ordinary play as the articulation of infantile relationships with primary objects. The room, the furniture, the various kinds of toys provided, and the analyst herself constitute the clinical frame—the "magic circle," which repeats symbolically the interiority of the mother–infant matrix—in which this transpires.

What Klein's work demonstrated was that there can be no psychoanalytic theory of play without reconsidering the practice of psychoanalysis and the nature of the clinical frame itself. What kind of space is this? In "Remembering, repeating, working through," Freud

(1914g) had already described transference as a playground: "We admit [unconscious fantasy] into the transference as a *playground* in which it is allowed to expand in almost complete freedom [...] The transference thus creates *an intermediate region* between illness and real life through which the *transition* from the one to the other is made" (p. 154; emphases added). Transference is a playground on or within which the emergence of unconscious fantasy is made possible and encouraged (Steingart, 1983; Sanville, 1991; Coen, 2005). Interpretation makes it possible for a patient to begin to tolerate the encounter with aspects of himself that he would rather split off. The more the patient is able to do this, the more interpretation assumes a transformative power. Psychoanalysis hinges on an ability not just to enjoy but to tolerate the seriousness of play.

As a "playground" and an "intermediate region" for "transition," the general field of transference constitutes what Winnicott conceives as that space "between" the subject and the external world from which subjectivity distinguishes itself. This intermediary reality *qua* "potential space" is not a space *of* potential, but is rather an area of experience that is *potentially* spatial—on its way to being a space, but not yet a space, and not yet distinct or fully differentiated from time. We might equally speak of "potential time," as the qualifier "potential" indicates a kind of experience where space and time have yet to be completely distinguished. That is, potential space, as a space of transition, is neither a space nor a time classically conceived but potentially either and both, situated at the transition—the "dimensionless and durationless borderline"—between the two. This potential or transitional space-time is the site of what Winnicott calls "playing":

> I make my idea of play concrete by claiming that *playing has a place* and a time. It is not *inside* by any use of the word [...]. Nor is it *outside*, that is to say, it is not part of the repudiated world, the not-me, that which the individual has decided to recognize (with whatever difficulty and even pain) as truly external, which is outside magical control. To control what is outside one has to *do* things, not simply think or wish, and *doing things takes time*. Playing is doing. (1971, p. 41)

> The essential feature of my communication is this, that playing is an experience, always a creative experience, and it is an experience in the space-time continuum, a basic form of living. (ibid., p. 50)

The achievement of developmental autonomy is oriented towards establishing an effective position within space and time, which allows for an experience of what Winnicott calls "creativity." Most of the pathologies with which Winnicott was concerned reflect failures in this area. His conception of analysis accordingly was as an engagement with a level of experience in which subjects and objects cannot be so rigorously distinguished. In his developmental thinking, he attempted to formulate this area in terms of "being":

> In the course of the emotional development of the individual a stage is reached at which the individual can be said to have become a unit. In the language that I have used this is a stage of "I am" [...] and (whatever we call it) the stage has significance because of the need for the individual to reach *being* before *doing*. "I am" must precede "I do," otherwise "I do" has no meaning for the individual. (p. 130)

"Being" reflects the child having become a subject, which is the condition of possibility—yet without having preceded—its relationships with the environment. With the establishment of "I am,"

> A new capacity for object-relating has now developed, namely, one that is based on an interchange between external reality and samples from the personal psychic reality. This capacity is reflected in the child's use of symbols and in creative playing and [...] in the gradual ability of the child to use cultural potential in so far as it is available in the immediate social environment. (p. 131)

This passage must be read against the background of Klein's account of the transition from the paranoid-schizoid position to the depressive position. What precedes Klein's depressive position is not, for Winnicott, anything like the world Klein portrays in terms of the paranoid-schizoid position; the latter describes pre-depressive functioning retroactively, in terms that belong to the depressive position having already been achieved. Klein's account of paranoid-schizoid phenomena is only what primitive experience looks like once the depressive position has been acceded to. Winnicott indicates that this is not a faithful account of the infant's early, pre-subjective experience: "Projective and introjective identifications both stem from this place where each is the same as the other" (1971, p. 80). Object relations are relations of identification; where there is no identification, there is no identity, but only "a bundle of projections" (p. 88; cf. p. 81). In the absence of the achievement of "being," object relations are characterized by an essential emptiness because the subject lacks "the capacity to be alone," as the capacity not just to be *alone*, but to *be* alone: To be oneself, by oneself, *as* oneself. This capacity characterizes not object relations, but what Winnicott calls "object usage" (p. 88). The ability to use an object reflects an openness to the object as genuinely other, not simply as a mirror image of the ego that can only receive projections and from which can only be extracted identifications.

Projection and introjection presuppose a subject, an agency that carries out these psychical operations. This may be a rudimentary ego structure, but as such it presents as an essentially closed, self-contained unit—something that insinuates itself as present from birth. This implies that the clinical relationship can in principle be approached from an external position where rational self-reflection is always, if at times only minimally, at work. The Kleinian infant is born into the world already as a unit—a very primitive unit, but bearing the form of unity fundamentally and from the beginning. This is why projecting and introjecting are from birth activities that the Kleinian infant-subject can *do*. For Winnicott, predepressive experiencing is not about doing, it is about being. To think this in terms of projection and introjection indicates a revision of presubjective experience from the register of the depressive, whole subject.

As evocative as Winnicott's thinking here may be, there is an ambiguity inherent to the relationship between being and doing as Winnicott portrays it. His basic point is that being precedes doing. Being, however, is not a given, it is an achievement. Winnicott spent his entire career exploring what happens when there is failure at this achievement, such that patients manifest an empty set of doings without a substantial sense of being as support. What this indicates is that, despite the necessity that being precede doing—and again, Winnicott knew very well that this is not a necessity, that empty doing is possible, if not prevalent these days—being itself is not primary in an ordinary existential sense. If being ("I am") is a "stage" that must be "reached," this means that there is something before being. This would not be a purely subjective, internal position, prior to a relation to external objects; rather, what is before being would constitute a dimension prior to anything like subjects or objects or any opposition between them. To speak like Winnicott for a moment: What could there be before being? What is an infant before it is?

The three terms that anchor Winnicott's thinking here are being, doing, and playing. It would seem that playing ought to be situated between being and doing, as the site of transition from the one to the other, through which the child must pass in order that her subjectivity (her "being") may become an effective and meaningful agent in the world (able to "do things"). If being is to precede doing, so that doing can have meaning, transitional phenomena would indicate an intermediate region between them, where being is a kind of doing, and the reverse. Playing may be doing then, but it is equally being. Playing is a kind of doing that is not distinct from being, a kind of doing that being *is*. How are we to think about something before being? This is precisely what Winnicott's expanded notion of "playing" attempts to describe. There is something before being, before doing, something that the opposition of being and doing works to conceal, and that Winnicott's concept of "playing," along with all the other terms that fall under its umbrella (transitional objects, not-me possessions, potential space/time) attempt to work out. One of the most powerful articulations of this idea is Winnicott's famously provocative statement, "There is no such thing as an infant" (1960, p. 39).

That "being precedes doing" is, admittedly, not such an astonishing thought. With "there is no such thing as an infant," we are in uncharted territory. There is something before being, before doing, and therefore prior to and from out of which the distinction between being and doing emerges. With the advent of his being, the child arrives at a position from which he is able to announce: "'Here I am. What is inside me is me and what is outside me is not me'" (Winnicott, 1971, p. 130). Prior to this, before the coordination of the inside and the outside in terms of a reliable opposition, the child is not able to say, "Here I am"—space and time ("here"), subjectivity ("I") and being ("am") have not yet coalesced into dynamic integration, and without such integration none of these terms has any stable referent. Before being able to assert, "Here I am," there are no relations between subjects and objects, only a kind of pure or potential relationality. This is why there is no such thing as an infant: The mother–infant relationship is not a dyad, nor is it simply a unity. Rather, it is relationality itself that is original and primary:

> What does the baby see when he or she looks at the mother's face?
> I am suggesting that, ordinarily, what the baby sees is himself or herself. In other words the mother is looking at the baby and *what*

she looks like is related to what she sees there. All this is too easily taken for granted. (1971, p. 112)

The infant's pre-subjective experience is to be understood here as fundamentally *pre*-subjective—not yet involving the categories of subject and object. Rather, the baby's existence is constitutively relational—it *is* the relationship to maternal care—before being a subject that can relate itself to objects, however primitive. That "there is no such thing as an infant" does not simply indicate that the baby can only survive physically and psychologically in relation to its mother; it means that the baby *is* this relation, before being anything like a subject whose relating to objects constitutes for it an activity—something a being does. "There is no such thing as an infant" because the infant is a relation prior to its being a subject, before submitting to the opposition of subjects and objects, having nothing yet to do with any such categories.

If playing is understood as a *before* that constitutes a link *between* being and doing, Winnicott's sense of "playing" begins to approximate Nietzsche's concept of "playing," itself a take on Heraclitus's sense of "becoming"—of "eternity as a child at play." Where becoming is accorded primacy, the opposition between being and doing—between self and action—needs to be revaluated. Nietzsche calls this a "terrible, paralyzing thought," in that it is only accessible via intuition, defying the Aristotelian conditions of formal logic. What is "terrifying, paralyzing" is the exit from metaphysics: The abandonment of conditions of certainty, knowledge, and substantial ground in favor of the playful affirmation of non-metaphysical indetermination, both psychologically and ontologically.

Formless experience and the fundamental rule

There are certainly limits to the comparisons that can be made between the patient/analyst and mother/infant relationships—limits of which Winnicott was perhaps too often in excess. If an analysis is to make it possible for the patient to "do things," this cannot be because "playing," as a clinical activity, depends on the analyst functioning in anything like a parental role. "Playing" describes not the transformation of being into doing, but the possibility of establishing one's being (a subject, a self) in such a way that doing can be done in a meaningful way. This takes *time*: "Playing and cultural experience are things that we do value in a special way; these link the past, the present, and the future; *they take up time and space*. They demand and get our concentrated deliberate attention, deliberate but without too much of the deliberateness of trying" (Winnicott, 1971, p. 109; emphasis in original). Analysis itself is essentially a kind of "taking up" of time and space: The patient commits to coming to a particular place four or five times a week, to disclosing his thoughts, to paying the fee, etc., but without the deliberateness of "trying to figure himself out." For Winnicott, analysis involves not being deliberate about such an activity, "taking up time and space" instead without purpose and with abandon.

That analysis should be understood in such a way was first formulated as a question of clinical technique in terms of the practice of free association. Of all Freud's innovations, free association has enjoyed a unique and peculiar fate. Subject neither to criticism nor revision, it has largely retreated into the background of contemporary analytic discourse. We take it for granted that new generations of analysts should understand why patients are to be encouraged to say whatever comes to mind instead of insistently trying to understand themselves. To rehearse what is involved in the practice of free association would hardly seem worthy of our attention, as if it advocated nothing controversial, nothing that challenges our most basic assumptions about the relationship between mind and world. I believe this is a serious mistake, and that thinking about Freud's historically innovative technical procedures in the light of Winnicott's understanding of the nature of the clinical relationship—and against the background of Nietzsche's critique of metaphysics—could lead to major reconsiderations of what psychoanalysis has to offer in the busy marketplace of available therapies today.

The neutrality of analytic listening depends on a capacity for "freely floating" or "evenly hovering" attention, as a way of obviating what the patient consciously intends to indicate, in favor of attending to the *potential* meanings inherent in what is actually said. For an analytic process to occur, the patient must let himself go to the "drift" of his associations, while the analyst must "catch" the patient's associations in such a way that they are not determined by preexisting ideas about what ought to be discovered (Bollas, 2002). When two people agree to engage in such a relationship, they are not just agreeing to do something that is socially unacceptable, they are actively experimenting with what it means to express oneself and with what it means to be a self capable of self-expression. Psychoanalysis is in this sense an experimental practice, it is not a formal procedure—it is a playing, not a doing.

Free association is an effort to abandon oneself to talking to an other one does not already know, about a self that has not been absolutely predetermined. By exercising an evenly hovering attention in the course of listening to a patient's speech, the analyst, rather than simply ignoring what the patient intends to mean, demonstrates a receptive capacity that discovers continuities of meaning (Kris, 1982) where these are intended to remain hidden: in those words and ideas that seem so familiar, so unimportant and not worth tending to. By exercising a capacity for neutral reverie, the analyst is able to associate to and to expand upon her own reactions to the patient's material, for the purpose of ascertaining those unconscious elements that insistently repeat themselves. By assuming that what the patient consciously intends is not at all what is essentially communicated in what is said, the analyst who follows her own associative pathways is able to hear what the patient cannot bear to hear in himself. To do this is neither to reveal the contents or the defensive structure of the patient's unconscious, nor is it to point out how the patient repeats the past of his childhood in the present of the treatment. Rather, as for Winnicott, analysis intends:

> [...] to afford opportunity for formless experience, and for creative impulses, motor and sensory, which are the stuff of playing. And on the basis of playing is built the whole of man's experiential existence. No longer are we either introvert or extrovert. We experience life in the area of transitional phenomena, in the exciting interweave of subjectivity and objective observation, and in an area that is intermediate between the inner reality of the individual and the shared reality of the world that is external to individuals. (1971, p. 64)

Analysis is an effort at allowing for the emergence of "formless experience"—that is, experience upon which has yet to be imposed rigid oppositions between inside and outside, subjectivity and objectivity, self and other. The effort to free associate maintains the analytic frame as just such a space and time in which meaning can be insisted upon and expanded. The more the analyst can suspend judgment about what the patient "really means," the more space the patient is afforded to explore the ways in which her experience can possibly be symbolized. The insistent pressure of unconscious wishes attempts to close this space down, and to express this reduction in the form of an unthinkable and obvious surface from which awareness and discussion are immediately deflected. This deflection often takes the form of a power struggle, in which the analyst attempts to tell the patient what he thinks is going on, either in the patient's life or in the treatment, and the patient generally accepts or refuses this. Analyses that proceed in this manner may just as likely be abandoned as go on forever, because they fail to "take up time and space" in an essential way.

For Winnicott, the evolution of an interpretable transference depends upon both participants rigorously abandoning themselves to purposelessness. Pre-calculated purpose on the part of either patient or analyst indicates resistance in the context of clinical play (Winnicott, 1971, p. 55). The counterpart to the patient's associations is not the analyst's interpretations—free association and interpretation are not related to one another in the form of questions and answers. Treatment conceived in this way reflects the form of an object relationship, in which the patient says what comes to mind, and the analyst tells the patient what it all means. Clinical play consists in the analyst responding to the patient's free associations with free associations of her own, recognizing and responding to connections as they surface in the patient's material by means of an evenly hovering attention. Of course, this cannot be what is always going on in the analytic relationship, but it is at these "ideal points" (Rosegrant, 2005) that Winnicott situates the mutative value of an interpretive approach.

Interpretation and transference

When the patient is free associating and the analyst is exercising an evenly hovering attention—or, if one prefers, what has come to be called, following Bion (1962/1984a), "reverie"—transference and countertransference phenomena are properly transitional phenomena: belonging to a realm in which subject and object, inside and outside, are not formally distinguishable, existing in their absolute forms only potentially. In the intermediate, transitional region that is transference, interpretive exploration of unconscious phantasy constitutes a form of play that gives back to the patient the time that has so far been absorbed by his suffering. Such exploration can have no precedent, it cannot be calculated in advance or managed either practically or theoretically:

> This interpreting by the analyst, if it is to have an effect, must be related to the patient's ability *to place the analyst outside the area of subjective phenomena*. What is then involved is the patient's ability to use the analyst [...]. In teaching, as in the feeding of a child, the capacity to use objects is taken for granted, but in [analytic] work it is necessary for us to be concerned with the development and establishment of the capacity to use objects and to recognize a patient's inability to use objects, where this is a fact. (Winnicott, 1971, p. 87; emphasis in original)

If analysis is not like teaching or feeding, this is because it is not an imparting of a substantial knowledge that has so far remained outside the patient's capacity for conscious self-awareness. To understand analysis as play is to think of the analytic situation otherwise than as a relationship between subjects and their objects. Of course, at the most banal level, an analysis is a relationship between two people. But this relationship, in which one person speaks indiscriminately while the other half-listens while monitoring herself, is not like any other. Playful interpretation is not possible in the context of an ordinary object relationship; it can only facilitate transformation where the patient is able, again in Winnicott's sense, to use the analyst, and where the analyst is able to present herself as the potential for difference, novelty, and change. This requires that we abandon all pretensions to having mastered an objective knowledge (Winnicott, 1971, pp. 86–87). Where treatment is conceived solely in terms of object relations, it makes little sense that interpretation could be effective as a therapeutic technique. If interpretation is effective as a therapeutic technique, this would indicate that the clinical relationship is not a relationship between intrinsically opposed subjects and objects, but something rather more playful:

> Interpretation outside the ripeness of the material is indoctrination and produces compliance. A corollary is that resistance arises out of interpretation given outside the area of the overlap of the patient's and the analyst's playing together. Interpretation when the patient

has no capacity to play is simply not useful, or causes confusion. (ibid., p. 51)

Clinical example

A patient (D) who had recently decided to move from a twice per week psychotherapy to a four times per week analysis was talking about how much it had already helped her coming to analysis, especially those weeks when she actually managed to make it to my office more than twice. D insisted that the structure and the rhythm (space and time) of our appointments helped her to organize her life, making her feel better and generally more stable. I said that an analysis is not just about structure and stability, it is also about intimacy—the intimacy that can only come with our seeing each other at least four times per week. I indicated further that what we had been doing was not analysis—not, as she believed, because she did not yet use the couch but instead continued to sit upright in the chair, but because although we had agreed to meet four days a week, not a week had gone by since we had arrived at that agreement where she had actually made it to four sessions. She complained that she had problems with intimacy, and that this was what the work we had done together so far had revealed to her. I asked D what she meant by "problems with intimacy." She said she couldn't quite describe it, but she gave an example. Some nights ago, she was feeling lonely and wanted male companionship. She called a male friend who invited her over to watch a movie. This man, she said, was "just a friend," he had a girlfriend, yet he and my patient were always very physical together. This, she said, was exactly what she had been looking for: physical intimacy with the clear indication that sex was not an option. When she got to his apartment, she was shocked to find the friend's girlfriend there, and thought of leaving immediately, but stayed anyway. At one point during the evening, the girlfriend went into the bedroom to make a phone call, at which point D moved from the chair she was sitting in, onto the couch where her male friend was, laying her head in his lap. This, she explained, was precisely the intimacy she wanted, but which had made her anxious, and of which she was still in some way afraid. So, I asked her what she was afraid would happen when she moved from the chair to the couch. She breezed through an answer that did not address the question, until I had the opportunity to ask it again, in modified form, but repeating her words concerning the move *from the chair to the couch.* Suddenly she became anxious and perplexed. She said she wasn't sure if I was talking about the previous night with her friend, or about what was going on in the room between us.

It is impossible not to hear the transference in this vignette. The move from the chair to the couch could not have been more explicitly linked to the question of treatment, although the patient had not heard it initially, nor had she consciously intended to indicate this. I could have said something like, "You speak of moving from the chair to the couch with your friend, but I wonder if you're not really talking about moving from the chair to the couch here with me?"—something that would have indicated directly the obvious link between the two situations. To have done so, however, would have been to establish a link that in fact severed the connection between the two possibilities, by implicitly asking the patient to choose between them, as if they were alternatives. Of course, in the immediacy of the moment, I had my own content-oriented associations about the patient's competitiveness with regard to the girlfriend, about her efforts to seduce both her friend and myself, and about how these defensively concealed the intensity of her need. An authoritarian impulse might therefore insist that, when I simply repeated her words, she understood what I "really meant," even if this was only implicit. This misses the point of the intervention by reducing interpretation of transference to the power of suggestion. Transference here consists in the fact that, unconsciously for D, moving to the couch with her friend and with me are the same (yet not identical). To interpret this in such a way as to force these possibilities apart would be to collapse the space of meaning in which the patient subsequently found herself, in which the excessive meaningfulness of her statements could be encountered as a function of the clinical environment itself, and about which she could begin to ask questions. Her sudden uncertainty about what I meant became an uncertainty about what she meant, and from there we were able to create more meaning by exploring the possibilities that had been opened up. My having simply repeated the words "from the chair to the couch" made it possible for her to hear their resonance in terms of our relationship, given how explicit and on the surface this already was. When she then said that she wasn't sure whether I was commenting on the story about the previous night with her friend or on her feelings about starting an analysis, she was speaking from a position well within the potential space of transitional, transferential "overlap." Her anxious perplexity was not the "confusion" that Winnicott warned of; it indicated rather that she had registered the ambiguity of her own speech, as something in excess of any subjective intention. This could not be addressed directly if it was to be sustained. One cannot comment *on* or *about* transference as "formless experience" without losing its transformative potential.

Symbolization, uncertainty, illusion

By emphasizing the undecidable ambiguity that all efforts at communication inevitably contain, the analyst is able to maintain and to expand what Freedman (1998) called "symbolizing space." For Winnicott, the clinical relationship externalizes the inner space of symbolization as the potential space of transference. This is to say that, where treatment consists in an "overlap of two areas of playing" (Winnicott, 1971, p. 39)—that is, where patient and analyst *are* playing—interpretation is not simply an activity that one might classify alongside other possible therapeutic techniques. Rather, the analytic relationship is itself a form of interpretation, as the space and time taken up together between the two participants, who do not present themselves to one another as subjects or objects (by ignoring the imperatives of ordinary social discourse), but perspectivally as mutually implicated, interpretive processes. The usefulness of interpretation as a therapeutic technique is otherwise problematic, as Winnicott indicates, outside the context of a relationship that is not itself constitutively interpretive. An analysis is not taking place when a subject is explaining himself to an object.

To pose questions that demand answers, or that imply something like a correct answer is possible, is to limit the space for questioning and for interpretive expansion. Such interpretations are indeed common: "You are treating me as if I ..." which, as Laplanche and Pontalis (1968) indicate, always carries with it an implicit, "... and you know very well that I am not really what you think I am" (p. 2). To interpret in this way is to privilege actuality over possibility, objectivity over meaning. While many would wish to claim that today such interventions are rare, unfortunately they are not. In many quarters, authoritarian forms of interpretation have largely not been replaced by more nuanced attunements, but have been reformulated to appear more palatable. For example, were one to say to a patient, "It's as if you feel your very existence is under attack here," this can sound like a very measured, caring reflection on the patient's immediate experience; nonetheless, it implicitly contains the suggestion that the patient *should not* feel this way. This is not due to any failure on the part of the analyst, but because it is formulated from the position of a subject talking to an object—it is a representative statement *about* the patient's experience, rather than an interpretive disclosure *of* the patient's experience. Even when formulated most empathically, in order to reveal to the patient his distortions while not intending to pass judgment, interventions such as these may constitute a way of saying, "You are distorting reality, but do not worry, that is perfectly normal ..." There may be instances in which just such an intervention is called for, but understanding when and where this is the case demands that analysts be more sensitive to how their most well-intentioned comments can inhibit the analytic process because they contain metaphysical prejudices about the nature of the relationship between mind and world. This is where Winnicott's thinking, like Nietzsche's, can be most helpful.

At times, to speak within the transference as a subject would speak to an object would be like actually telling a child that his transitional object is not really created by him but is externally discovered. No good-enough parent would ever dream of saying such a thing, but a well-meaning parent might think it appropriate to say something that amounts to, "Your transitional object is both created by you and discovered in the outside world. And that is fine, you do not have to choose which one is real." Of course, this is itself a way of posing questions that Winnicott insists must not be posed with regard to transitional phenomena. The question that must never be posed to the child concerning his transitional object is whether that object is something he has discovered in the outside world or something he has created from out of himself. According to Winnicott, it is crucial that this question never even be *formulated* (1971, p. 12). The problem with this question is not its content, but its form: Its traumatizing potential is due to the fact that it imposes a structure of opposition on the child's organization of reality, forcing him to take up a position within this structure prematurely. Such an imposition is equally restrictive when it is introduced into clinical process. Rodman (2003) quotes Susanna Isaacs having said of Winnicott, "he knew that you could only disturb people by trying to force knowledge on them" (p. 47).

One way of thinking about this would be to say that transferential, transitional phenomena cannot be interpreted positively. For Winnicott, interpreting transference as play means not deciding what the patient is "really talking about," consciously or unconsciously, since interpretation here intends not to determine but to hold open the space in which more meaning always might be generated. A statement along the lines of, "I wonder if you don't feel with me the same way you describe feeling with your wife?"—again, even when most carefully, thoughtfully, and accurately posed—is not properly a question but an effort to force the patient into a position of deciding what he is going to consider reality; it does not address the transference symbolically, but rather collapses its symbolizing potential. Any such position *on* or *about* transference implicitly carries the indication that this is not real, because it is not shared. Transference can be conceived as that dimension of experience in which oppositions between, and final decisions about, subjects and objects, inside and outside, past and present cannot be arrived at. To treat any absolute distinction between past and present as if it were real and not a fantasy misses the opportunity to examine what emerges in this transitional area where one does not quite know what one is saying, but it seems exceedingly meaningful nonetheless.

To interpret transference as play is to maintain its transformative potential by speaking ambiguously and without certainty, so that transferential experiences are provided the opportunity for symbolization. Symbolization precludes positive knowledge. A symbolizing position cannot lend itself to an experience of rigid cognitive certainty, as it is inherently playful and indefinite, allowing for multiple meanings and always for further interpretation. To say something like, "You are experiencing me like you have always experienced your mother," or, "It must be difficult for you to tell me about these things," is to speak as a subject of certainty and knowledge—as a being that is doing something—which is not, for Winnicott, what it means to be in the transference. These interventions seemingly belong to different clinical approaches, but they articulate two sides of the same instructive, objectivizing coin. To intervene from a position that does not share in the illusion of transference is precisely not to ask questions, but instead to demand that the patient choose sides in a series of either/or oppositions. This is not simply coercive, it fails to appreciate how transferential, transitional phenomena challenge commonsense notions about subjectivity, objectivity, and the relationship between them. In the contemporary analytic literature, this failure is reflected both in a classical, "one person" effort at educating the patient about the contents of his unconscious, as well as in intersubjectivist, "two person" approaches that seek to draw out of the patient the truth of his conscious experience in terms of an ongoing dialogue. Both of these approaches, from a Winnicottian perspective, as this can be seen to have been anticipated in certain regards by Nietzsche, effectively refuse to engage with transference symbolically—that is, in terms of will to power—by continuing to think in terms of, and thereby to impose, metaphysical structures of opposition.

On this account, transference appears to be more than just a mechanism according to which patients impose figures from their pasts onto currently real relationships. Transference is not a distortion of reality to be corrected either by instruction or empathy from a position of objectivity and knowledge occupied by the analyst. Rather, within the transferential field, the patient *is* this distortion, and must be engaged with accordingly. This is not something that might be remedied, and even our most genuinely empathic interventions can conceal just such an aim. Where treatment is conceived as playing, unconscious phantasies are not psychological contents one "has," the enactment of which constitutes an activity one "does." Rather, patient and analyst *are* unconscious fantasy together in the form of the primitive ("formless") relationality articulated as the transference/countertransference matrix. Interpretation consists in disclosing this, so that illusion can be integrated as a positive juncture. The interpretive relationship in this sense exists then not "in" the intermediate region between being and doing, but *as* this intermediate region or this transitional relationality. What Winnicott introduces is a way of thinking about clinical experience such that our concepts of treatment and of transference, interpretation and relationship, patient and analyst begin to coincide, which is not to say they lose all distinction. As potential space-time or as transitional phenomenon, transference must be interpreted intransitively, which is to say that it would seem inadequate to speak of "*the* transference," as if this were itself some object, some circumscribed event from which one could effectively abstract oneself, and that could be managed then by means of an increased capacity for self-mastery through conscious reflection.

Experience

According to Alan Schrift (1990), "Play is a Nietzschean theme in a twofold sense: It operates in his thinking both as a stylistic device and as a philosophical 'concept'" (p. 63). That is, Nietzsche both writes *about* play, and he does so *playfully*—which is not to say without rigor, but in a way that takes its concept as its stylistic guide in order to think new thoughts in novel ways, to play with thinking at the level of "intuition" linked to experiencing rather than subordinated to abstract rules of non-contradiction. The same could be said of Winnicott, and both Winnicott and Nietzsche have as a result often won the disapproval of those incapable of "slow reading," in that they "reduce to despair every sort of man who is 'in a hurry'" (Nietzsche, 1881/1997b, p. 5). Both Nietzsche and Winnicott aspire to a kind of thinking and of experiencing capable of "taking time, becoming still" thoroughly at odds with the relentless liberation of drives that characterizes the modern world. Nietzsche's efforts at doing so are philosophical in nature, whereas Winnicott's are clinical; when read together they indicate most powerfully the point at which philosophical and clinical concerns intersect.

In an essay that addresses Freud but in which Nietzsche's influence is pervasive, Sarah Kofman (1983/2007) writes:

> When the patient addresses the analyst and eagerly awaits a response, there is nothing more shocking and painful than silence coming from the other side of the couch. However, the lack of response on the analyst's part is essential for the radical transformation of the patient's relation to language: for getting the patient to stop using language as an instrument of communication, of exchange and dialogue, and to start speaking "for the sake of speaking," without a purpose and without expecting a response. To recover, then, is to be capable of becoming indifferent to the speech of the other, to be capable of detaching oneself from it in order to play on own one's, while still in the other's presence. (p. 60)

Going on to cite Winnicott on the role of play in figuring the child's "capacity to be alone," and recalling that the negotiation of this capacity had already been demonstrated by Freud in the famous *fort/da* scene of *Beyond the Pleasure Principle*, Kofman powerfully grasps how analytic clinical practice intersects with Nietzsche's attempt at a destruction of metaphysics:

> If the aim of analysis is this ludic detachment that enables the patient to send the analyst out for a long walk, then the "seriousness" of

> recovery is no longer opposed to play, and play turns out to be a
> serious activity. In this way, Freud effaces the metaphysical opposi-
> tion between play and seriousness. (p. 61)

Effacing the metaphysical opposition between play and seriousness is
the orientation of Nietzsche's genealogical critique of morality as what
issues from the Platonic-Christian opposition between an eternal world
beyond associated with seriousness and truth, and the material world
of time, change, and becoming associated with illusion, frivolousness,
and ignorance. Whereas Freud's thinking more often than not falls well
within the province of metaphysics, the practice of interpretation that
he invents indicates a passage toward something much more radical
and transformative where the relationship between theory and practice, as that between seriousness and play, is concerned. What Nietzsche
accomplishes textually and in theory, Freud accomplishes clinically and
in practice. With Winnicott we can witness the beginnings of an integration of these two projects.

In an essay written in 1870 but unpublished in his lifetime, entitled,
"The Dionysiac world view," Nietzsche works out the basic premises
of his *The Birth of Tragedy*, published two years later. These concern the
relationship between the Greek deities Apollo and Dionysius, identified
respectively with the experiences of dream and intoxication, and with
the arts of sculpture and music. For both categories Nietzsche identifies two forms of play specific to each. With respect to the Apolline,
Nietzsche (1999) writes, "[…] whereas in dream the individual human
being plays with the real, the art of the image-maker (in the wider
sense) is a *playing with dream*" (p. 119). With respect to the Dionysian,
Nietzsche writes, "If intoxication is nature playing with human beings,
the Dionysiac artist's creation is a playing with intoxication" (p. 121).
In both cases art involves appropriations and reversals that reflect the
way in which the artist relates to experience. This depends upon a capacity for self-overcoming, which is to say for overcoming the everyday
opposition of self and world that generates resentment, stupidity, and
nihilism:

> […] the opposition of the subjective and the objective […] has no
> place in aesthetics, since the subject, the individual who wills and
> furthers his own egoistic purposes, can be considered only the
> adversary and not the origin of art. But in so far as the subject is

an artist, he is already liberated from his individual will and has become a medium through which the only truly existent subject celebrates his redemption through illusion. (p. 32)

It is tempting to read into this passage Winnicott's distinction between true and false selves, and not without good reason, for at the heart of Winnicott's reflections lay similar sentiments about the nature of the analytic process. Where analysis is conceived as an effort at playfully abandoning those strictures that govern life outside the consulting room, the opposition of the subjective and the objective has no place in the clinic. This would make psychoanalysis an attempt at overcoming metaphysics. Although Winnicott had no way of thinking what this might mean, his natural inclinations and curiosity seem to have oriented him in this profoundly Nietzschean direction.

CHAPTER FIVE

Nietzsche, Lacan, madness

> Parmenides said, "one cannot think of what is not"; —we are at the
> other extreme, and say "what can be thought of must certainly be
> a fiction."
>
> —Nietzsche, *The Will to Power*

On January 3rd, 1889, in the city of Turin, Nietzsche witnessed a man cruelly beating a horse. The man's living wage as a carriage-driver depended upon the well-being of the horse he was beating, and which he was able to claim legally as his own. The irrational cruelty exhibited was thus the expression of a purely suicidal intention articulating itself as if it were an enhancement of subjective agency—the very opposite of what Nietzsche had meant by "power." Nietzsche intervened, embraced the animal, and collapsed. Overcome by commercial culture—a then emergent cultural form that authorizes interpretations of life in terms of ownership, petty cruelty, and suicide—Nietzsche spent the next few days losing his mind. That he suffered from this process is not necessarily indicated by the historical accounts of this brief period in his life. His landlady is alleged to have peeped through his window one night and witnessed the famous author dancing and singing in the nude. She concluded that he must have been drunk on wine. Whether or not this was the case, it suggests that he was not suffering, but ecstatically enjoying himself. Nietzsche would spend the remaining eleven years of his life in a state of catatonic psychosis, paying the price for this transitory encounter with absolute enjoyment.

In his 1969–1970 seminar, published under the title, *The Other Side of Psychoanalysis* (1991/2007), Lacan attempted to situate what was specific to psychoanalysis within a broader historical and cultural context. This seminar was delivered at the time of Lacan's moving to the University of Paris at Vincennes, and he pursues the question of the relationship between the clinical field and the university. Whereas Freud (1937c) had grouped psychoanalysis and education together among the three "impossible professions," Lacan sought to demonstrate just how thoroughly different they are. Lacan always insisted that what is essential to analysis is the experience of the clinic, that even the most thorough familiarity with psychoanalytic theory remains a pretense without substance. Such a claim is anathema in the context of the university. It amounts to saying that one cannot know anything about psychoanalysis unless one has undergone an analysis, and from the perspective of the university's claim to universal knowledge this can only appear as (at best) an epistemological elitism, or (at worst) the foundations of a cult. Lacan admits that there is some truth to this, but he counters by arguing that this is no less true of what he calls the "discourse of the university." The discourse of the university—that is, what one pays for when one attends or delivers one's children off to college these days—prides itself on being unconcerned with the particularity of individual experience. As Lacan (1966/2006) indicates, the psychoanalytic clinic, unlike the university, does not intend to promote figures of mass individuation specific to market democracy (pp. 684–685). Psychoanalysis is not part of the service industry; it has no "students," "clients," or "consumers." Where it clings to a medical discourse in continuing to refer to its "patients," this is only because "analysand" remains too unfamiliar to those who find novelty intolerable.

For Lacan, what psychoanalysis teaches is not the same as what can be learned from pedagogy. Unlike the discourse of the university, the analytic discourse cannot be understood as a relationship between a master and a disciple through which an eternally self-identical, objective knowledge is seamlessly, procedurally transmitted. Psychoanalysis and education are founded on radically different principles; they constitute thoroughly different discourses or forms of relation. The university makes available an approach to knowledge as something that is essentially and everywhere the same for everyone: everyone who pays the same, attends the same, and learns the same. Psychoanalysis, to the contrary, makes available a form of knowledge that is specific to the patient herself, and in ways that generate tradition at the level of the individual, rather than at the level of the collective. What is at stake in an analysis, Lacan argues, isn't the truth about the world to which one must adjust oneself, but the truth about the analysand's unique experience or interpretation of the world—in Lacanian terms: the encounter with jouissance.

For Lacan, psychoanalysis is not a university discourse; for Nietzsche, neither is philosophy. Nietzsche never tired of distancing himself from "the great majority of industrious scholars and the other accessories of the universities" (1886/1989a, p. 70). The university system had initially embraced Nietzsche, awarding him a professorship in philology at the young age of twenty-four, but it quickly rejected him on the publication of *The Birth of Tragedy* for his deliberate refusal to conform to the established rules of academic propriety. In *Beyond Good and Evil*, Nietzsche writes:

> It is especially the sight of those hodgepodge philosophers who call themselves "philosophers of reality" or "positivists" that is capable of injecting a dangerous mistrust into the soul of an ambitious young scholar: These are at best scholars and specialists themselves—that is palpable—they are all losers who have been *brought back* under the hegemony of science, after having desired *more* of themselves at some time without having had the right to this "more" and its responsibilities—and who now represent, in word and deed, honorably, resentfully, and vengefully the *unbelief* in the masterly task and masterfulness of philosophy. (ibid., p. 123)

What are we to make of this statement? Is this a bit of *ressentiment* on the part of Nietzsche himself? To say of professional scholars and specialists that "they are all losers"—is this an instance of Nietzsche's style or of his pathology? Perhaps it indicates an intrinsic relation between the two: What links style and pathology, and which can be swiftly rejected in the call for quantifiable "facts" or comfortably neutralized and embraced as mere "subjective opinion." Freud, it should be recalled, also aspired to a university position in neurology, but was denied this opportunity given the pervasive anti-Semitism of turn of the century Austria, without which psychoanalysis might never have been invented. That the academy that had historically rejected both Nietzsche and Freud has since clamored to integrate itself with Nietzschean and Freudian discourse—cyclically repudiating efforts to do so and then again reinvesting in them, over and over—reflects the commercialization of knowledge, which is part and parcel of the naturalization of science as metaphysics. Nietzsche and Freud are in this way reduced to being purveyors of fashionable academic theory. Reflecting on the consequences of this reduction, Alenka Zupančič (2003) writes:

> Why is it absolutely unimaginable (among contemporary Nietzscheans themselves) that someone would use this kind of "style" and write, for instance, "XY, the well-known professor of cultural studies, is a fat cow with a fine style"? This is absolutely forbidden, and there is no poetic license that could make it acceptable to present-day academia. If Nietzsche's style is esteemed within academia, it is in no way accepted by it. (p. 3)

Academic institutions operate according to a logic in which what is accepted is not esteemed, and in which what is esteemed is not to be accepted (Deresiewicz, 2014). Nietzsche had perceived and suffered the effects of this logic. His vision of philosophy as a practice beyond mere scholarship led him to embrace experimentalism in style, and to practice textually in ways that would indicate the fault lines in all claims to universality. Of his projected "philosophers of the future," Nietzsche (1886/1989a) writes:

> [...] certainly they will be men of experiments. With the name in which I dared to baptize them I have already stressed expressly their attempts and delight in attempts: Was this done because as critics in body and soul they like to employ experiments in a new, perhaps wider, perhaps more dangerous sense? Does their passion for knowledge force them to go further with audacious and painful experiments than the softhearted and effeminate tastes of a democratic century could approve? (p. 134)

Experiments—not the accumulation of factual knowledge. In Nietzsche's beloved French, "experiment" is *expérience*. In dissociating psychoanalysis from the university, Lacan sought to ground the analytic experience outside classical conceptions of knowledge. The clinic is a site of experimentation, in which one cannot know and one cannot expect, in which, "we are wrong to expect, which is the difficulty of being an analyst" (Lacan, 1976/2013b, p. 8). Lacanian psychoanalysis is increasingly attracting the attention of clinicians in the English-speaking world because it is that form of psychoanalysis that has most rigorously dedicated itself to theorizing the analyst's experience of not-knowing, attempting to turn that experience into a clinically effective position. This is a direction that psychoanalysis must traverse if it is to survive the standardizing demands of the academic and mental health industries. Nietzsche is instrumental to this effort. The later phase of Lacan's work provides the best coordinates for a psychoanalytic appreciation both of Nietzsche's philosophy and of his madness. This is because the later Lacan refuses to consider these two projects as dissociable from one another. It is, in turn, Nietzsche who best allows us to assess what Lacan has to offer those who wish to respond to the crisis of the psychoanalytic clinic today. To appreciate this requires an effort first to distinguish between the earlier and the later orientations of Lacan's thinking.

Early Lacan

Lacan's 1958 essay, "The direction of the treatment and the principles of its power," is an attempt at describing what actually happens in analysis, as against all popular accounts circulating at the time. The appearance of the word "power" in its title records a moment in Parisian intellectual history when an encounter with Nietzsche was never far off, even if, as for Lacan, he was never explicitly a point of reference. At this point in his career, Lacan was thoroughly preoccupied with what was becoming established, mainstream psychoanalysis under the direction of the International Psychoanalytical Association. In the 1950s, both in Europe and America, psychoanalytic orthodoxy was once again wringing its hands over the dilemma of transference—that is, the charge of suggestion—much in the same way that Freud had struggled in his efforts to establish interpretation as a way of responding "objectively" to his patients' speech. The debate over countertransference emerged from out of this context when Paula Heimann published her paper, "On countertransference" (1950), in which she had thoroughly revaluated the concept. She was the first to say that countertransference is inevitable and must be treated not as the analyst's resistance but as providing information about the patient—further confounding what it means to speak of a distinction between subjective and objective facts in a clinical context. Heimann's paper and the debate that ensued mark the beginning of the debate, still to this day essential to the contemporary American interpersonal schools, over whether psychoanalysis is to be conceived as a "one person" or "two person" psychology.

Lacan rejects this approach entirely by describing the structure of the analytic relationship in terms of the quaternary structure of the game of bridge. He situates the analyst in the position of the dummy—*le mort*—who produces effects to the extent that he demonstrates a lack of understanding or willingness to produce. The analogy to *le mort* in bridge describes the analyst's role of occupying the Symbolic function of the dead father, informed by a lack of Being. The analyst thus places himself in the position of something that is lacking (Fink, 2004, pp. 5–11). From this position, the analyst is able to draw out the subject of desire. Desire can only be grasped through the play of signifiers as this emerges in the analysand's discourse. Signifiers are not only words but elemental bits of communication (including sounds, letters, gestures, etc.) that insistently repeat themselves and that give the analysand's discourse its unique particularity. This particularity is easily missed in everyday dialogue, the purpose of which appears to be the communication of agreeable, shared meaning. By refusing to assume that consciously intended meaning is immediately transparent, the analyst listens for the play of signifiers in order to open up the possibility of situating herself in the place of the Other, so that she can encourage symbolization of unconscious fantasy. This possibility is precluded where the analyst is acting out of her own demand, thereby failing to establish an ethical clinical relationship. According to Lacan, this is what happens in a cognitive or ego psychological approach to treatment. Where subjectivity is thought purely in terms of cognition, it makes little sense that interpretation could be effective as a therapeutic technique, without interpretation being reduced to explanation, and as a means of encouraging identification with the analyst's ego. To intervene at the level of the unconscious is to not be concerned with meaning but with what insists prior to and fixes meaning. Meaning belongs to consciousness as an after-effect of the combinatory play of signifiers that structures the unconscious. This is what it means to say, "the unconscious is structured like a language."

The subject of the unconscious fixates around a particular signifier which is itself unconscious. This is why Lacan speaks of the "subject of the signifier," and why "a signifier is what represents the subject for another signifier." The movement of the subject from one signifier to the next, even if that means from one symptom or form of suffering to another, is what constitutes health: the ability of the subject to remain fluid and to occupy different positions. According to Bruce Fink (1995):

> We can provisionally view symptoms as having such a substitu-
> tional structure, wherein the subject as meaning persists indefi-
> nitely in its subjugated state unless a new metaphor is achieved. In
> that sense, analysis can be viewed, in Lacan's theory, as requiring
> that new metaphors be forged. For each new metaphor brings with
> it a precipitation of subjectivity which can alter the subject's posi-
> tion. (p. 70)

Treating a symptom means opening up what is stuck at the level of fact by means of metaphorization or symbolization. In order to accomplish this, Lacan asks us to listen for those signifiers that repeatedly get stuck and that insistently crop up in the clinical material. Signification describes meaning as a form of fixation. A signifier that "has" meaning—*a* meaning—is captivated by fixed signification. When the signifier does not relate the subject to meaning, but rather determines meaning as representation, as what the ego intends or "means to say" in order to submit itself to the demands of the Other, neurosis has taken root. This is what holds the subject together, while at the same time obstructing the mobility of desire. In the analysis of neurosis, the analyst works to break up signification. The transference, which Lacan insists ought not be interpreted, holds the patient together by offering a provisional identity that will sustain him until a new mobility of desire can be constructed.

Le mort is Lacan's term for conceiving of analytic neutrality. This is a formally "paternal" position to the extent that it indicates an indifference to the subject of desire. It is an empty position that "knows" nothing but for that very reason is capable of drawing the subject of desire forth. To listen not to intentional meaning but to the patterns in the patient's discourse puts the analyst in the empty position of the dummy, keeping countertransference from interfering with the analyst's interventions by tending to the autonomy of the signifier. Lacan is not interested in the analyst's knowledge, as this keeps the analysis in the realm of the Imaginary, using the patient to justify the analyst's theoretical perspective. The analyst must instead assume the place of the Other, but in such a way that cannot be anticipated in advance. The analyst's skill—which is something altogether different from knowledge—consists in spontaneously taking advantage of those moments where it is not meaning and sense but a radical absence of articulable meaning and sense that reveals itself. For Lacan, it is not the cause but the absence of specifiable meaning that liberates. It is not the answer to the question "why?" but freedom from the metaphysical demands of causal questioning that psychoanalysis has to offer.

In "The Freudian thing, or the meaning of the return to Freud in psychoanalysis," Lacan famously takes up Freud's statement, "Wo es war, soll ich werden" (1966/2006, p. 347ff.). He makes much of the fact that Freud does not write, "Wo das Es war, soll das Ich werden," insisting that Freud is not talking here about the psychical agencies of the second topography. The absence of definite articles indicates for Lacan that Freud is describing not "the Ego and the Id," but the subject and the Other as ethically rather than as ontically determined. Lacan's French translation is: "Là où c'était, dois-je advenir." The temporality of this formula is crucial: "There where it *was*, should I *become*." The temporal dynamism implicit in this phrase indicates the development peculiar to analytic treatment; it does not imply the taming of one psychic agency by another. This is centrally important to Lacan's idea of a psychoanalytic ethics, and of the unconscious not as an ontical object but as an ethical injunction: "The status of the unconscious, which, as I have shown, is so fragile on the ontic plane, is ethical. In his thirst for truth, Freud says, *Whatever it is, I must go there*, because, somewhere, this unconscious reveals itself" (Lacan, 1973/1981, p. 33). Freud's "it" in this statement is not "the Id" as a specific psychic agency, but the Lacanian Other—an Other related to and designated purely as such, without determination in the form of another subject (unconscious, interpersonal, or otherwise). Lacan therefore interprets Freud's sentence to mean that the subject of the unconscious must arise from out of the Symbolic order, that is, the network of social relations, customs, and traditions. This was to challenge American ego psychology's interpretation of the formula— Wo es war, soll ich werden—as of Freudian practice itself, as promoting an understanding of treatment as a means of exerting power in the service of forcing adaptation to the status quo. This understanding remains more prevalent than the contemporary professional field would care to admit.

Rewriting the Freudian concept of the wish as desire, the early Lacan articulates an ethics of psychoanalysis and an authentic psychoanalytic practice through the Heideggerian question of Being, appropriated via Sartre and the French existentialist movement. Analysts who think their role in a medical or "mental health" context are, for Lacan, technocrats operating in accordance with a metaphysics of power and domination in the name of symptom reduction. Similarly, the dual relation patient/ analyst, thought in terms of efforts at identifying with a good object, belongs to the Imaginary register of opposition and competition. Lacan therefore argues that to consider countertransference solely in terms of affect is to move away from the early Freud, for whom affects belong to consciousness. Lacan does not abandon the theme of countertransference, rather he rewrites it in terms of the effects of the signifier: To be affected by the patient's discourse is not to empathize with the other as object, but to belong to a common order of the Symbolic as this is distributed at the level of speech. Countertransference, as those affects felt by the analyst in relation to and as an effect of the patient's speech, leaves us stuck at the level of the ego and the dual, mirroring relation of narcissism. For an analysis to be effective it must intervene at the level of the subject, not simply at the level of the psychological ego or self. The subject is the ground of all the patient's narcissistic identifications, expressed as self-images by means of the ego as what coordinates these images. This is where interpretation must intercede, as this ground is constituted as ground upon the child's entrance into the Symbolic order. What this means clinically is that an interpretation must not be an answer to a question, but an effort to hold open a space for questioning. An interpretation should not provide a solution, it should unravel the knot that is an unconscious identification.

For the early Lacan, the practice of interpretation intends to disclose lack as the condition of the analysand's discourse conceived symptomatically as addressed to the Symbolic Other. Interpretation does not reveal hidden signification but moves the relations between signifiers along. By encouraging free association, the analyst provides the analysand with the opportunity to pay no attention to effects of meaning but to keep relating one signifier to the next in order to indicate the absence or lack around which this effort endlessly circulates. Lack is thereby disclosed not as the absence of an object, but as the insurmountable failure of language in the effort fully to disclose who or what one is. Interpretation consists in acknowledging those moments in the patient's discourse when lack and the desire to escape it appear, in order to reveal Being itself as lack, castration as the condition of subjectivity. This is not the final truth of the analysand's discourse but what keeps it in motion, what sustains the effort always to keep saying more. Interpretation here is again not an explanation of the analysand's experience, a way of proffering him information about himself that he does not possess; it consists rather in highlighting those areas where language seems to fail yet meaning is intensive. These are the moments when the analysand has said more than he intended to say, when his speech or silence is recognizably overdetermined and opened upon more meaning than he had intended to let on about. These are the strange, anxious moments in which the analysand does not know what he is saying, but it appears exceedingly meaningful nonetheless. Lacking *a* meaning, speech appears meaning*ful* in a way that is itself meaning*less*. These moments reflect Being as what language cannot speak, where Being is the absence or lack that the subject figured by language is ultimately founded upon.

Nietzsche would have bristled at the early Lacan's insistence on Being and lack as yet another expression of the directives of Platonism and Christianity. Where truth is figured as castration, this enforces a nihilistic logic that opposes truth and illusion, installing lack *at* the center of Being rather than embracing a lack *of* Being, center, or ground. Lacan's so-called "structuralist phase," equally determined by his commitment to Sartre's existentialist project, represents an attempt to think psychoanalysis in terms of a nihilistic encounter with Being as the articulation of "nothingness" taken to be the truth of subjective experience. The circulation of signifiers in the subject's psychic economy was at this point conceived by Lacan as a structure or as a signifying pattern organized around Being as lack. When Derrida (1967/1978) wrote, "*Form* fascinates when one no longer has the force to understand force from within itself. That is, to create" (p. 4), his target was precisely just such an effort to think Being metaphysically as the presence of an absence. Nietzsche had already conceived this insistence as the orientation of *ressentiment* or the "spirit of revenge" as "faith in opposite values."

And yet, Lacan's preoccupation with the *play* of the signifying chain and with *becoming* brought him close to Nietzsche's conception of the possibility of a science beyond metaphysics. When Lacan turns, at the end of his teaching, away from the logic of the signifier (presence and absence) and toward what underwrites this logic in the form of the body and its relation to enjoyment or jouissance, he breaks with the fascination of structure or form as an index of Being and provides psychoanalysis with its most rigorous account of an encounter with finite becoming as the orientation of clinical practice. This leads Lacan in the end not only to dispense with the technocratic orientation of ego psychology, but to develop a concept of the unconscious as something other than a bar that eternally divides the subject from the body. The combinatory operation of the signifier is founded upon the auto-differentiating function of the body that speaks. This is the later Lacan's move away from the repression model of defense, which leads to an abandonment of the classical concept of the unconscious (even in the form that Lacan had given it as signifying chain), in favor of an approach to the body as what he calls "speaking-being" or *parlêtre*.

Later Lacan

The early Lacan is optimistic: Channel the patient's Imaginary constructions into the register of the Symbolic by assuming the position of the Other and everything will resolve itself. The later Lacan is not so optimistic. Adjusting to the shifting nature of his time, Lacan sees that by the late 1960s and early 1970s, the Symbolic order is no longer what it once was, and that in the context of a culture which celebrates unbridled self-expression, feeding meaning and signification leads to analysis interminable. The analyst who establishes himself in the place of *le mort*, thereby getting the analysand to speak without obsessive self-reflection, winds up supporting efforts to engender endless, meaningless discourse—meaningless to the extent that it pursues meaning without end, in such a way that invites new forms of narcissistic inertia. Lacan came to call this inertia the "blah blah blah," the flow of which the analyst should be able to interrupt, without having recourse to futile authoritarian efforts to convince the patient that the analyst's perspective is *right*: "One must not convince (*convaincre*). What is proper to psychoanalysis is not to vanquish (*vaincre*), regardless of whether people are stupid (*con*) or not" (1975/1998, p. 53; trans. modified). Toward the end of his career Lacan approached the possibility of clinical transformation in terms of the analysand's ability to encounter what constitutes his particular form of excessive enjoyment or jouissance— the way in which, outside his conscious understanding and in a way that threatens to annihilate his sense of self, he derives pleasure from his suffering. Jouissance is excessive in that it produces an experience of conscious pain and anxiety where unconsciously it functions as a source of exquisite pleasure, encouraging forms of enjoyment experienced as symptomatically structured repetitions in the absence of knowledge or understanding. Thus people present for analysis complaining, "I keep doing *x*, but I don't know *why*," as if obtaining the answer to this question would somehow magically change their behavior. Lacan came to see that in the context of contemporary culture—which had appropriated the logic of this complaint and had exploited it for commercial ends—analyses that were structured in this way would reinforce stagnation rather than move beyond it.

Lacan's early efforts were organized around encouraging patients to accept this position of not knowing (figured negatively as castration) as evidence of their finite existence, beyond the narcissistic dimension of the Imaginary. This dimension is possessed of its own particular jouissance, one that sustains what Nietzsche had called metaphysics. The jubilation of the child in front of the mirror is an Imaginary jouissance provided by the image of wholeness, integration, and totality. This form of enjoyment functions as an obstacle to Symbolic integration, leading to a conception of treatment as an effort at getting rid of the Imaginary and overcoming narcissism by liberating the vicissitudes of desire. With Nietzsche we might say that Lacan came to realize that in his early work he had failed to conceive of the relation between the Imaginary and the Symbolic in terms of play, disruption, or becoming, too preoccupied as he was with the category of Being construed as lack. What Nietzsche discovers in the Heraclitean "concept" (and here I put the word "concept" in quotes to indicate the extent to which it is intended to break with the order of conceptual understanding) of play, Lacan introduces in terms of the Real, which in his later work he increasingly comes to focus on. For Nietzsche, one does not formally escape narcissistic or Imaginary logics of opposition without affirming their ultimate meaninglessness as irreducible. To move beyond metaphysics is not to situate oneself impossibly "outside" classical logic, but to affirm the absurd meaninglessness of logic with laughter (Nietzsche) or as a source of enjoyment (Lacan).

In the later phase of his teaching, Lacan does not start with the primacy of Being and language, but with the primacy of jouissance. This is not a source of conscious, logical certainty, but on the contrary belongs to the living body as that which develops, changes, and becomes, indicating what is in excess of all relations to others conceived on the model of intersubjectivity. For the later Lacan, what is at issue in the clinic is no longer a subject that addresses, solicits, or seduces, but a living body that enjoys. What is important for the treatment is not the structured patterns of signification but the illocutionary event of vocalization. What the later Lacan therefore presses us to listen to in the clinical encounter is not a subject that communicates to an Other, but a body that enjoys all by itself, producing meaning meaninglessly in an effort both to indicate and to conceal its status as solitary and alone. By circumscribing this dimension of experience and attempting to intervene where all possibilities for relation seem contra-indicated, Lacan offers a way of thinking beyond intersubjectivity and a way of intervening in terms of what Nietzsche had called "force": beyond good and evil, beyond subject and object, beyond all logics of opposition provided by philosophy as metaphysics and by psychoanalysis where it cannot encounter itself on its own terms but instead insistently repeats figures of narcissistic demand.

In his *Seminar XX—Encore*—Lacan (1975/1998) asked his audience, "What is jouissance?" He answered, "Here it amounts to no more than a negative instance [...] Jouissance is what serves no purpose (*ne sert à rien*)" (p. 3). This would not have been a definition expected by those committed members of his audience at the time. For decades Lacan had insisted that the function of jouissance was to bind the subject to the signifier: To create via language a relation between the child and the world to which it must adapt itself without having had any say in the contours of its creation. Although Lacan's thinking about jouissance had changed dramatically over the course of his seminars, jouissance had always been conceived as a product of the encounter of the subject with language, as an effect of the signifier on a body driven to accommodate the demands of the Other. The later Lacan does not derive jouissance from the relationship between the subject and language; jouissance becomes rather that which pre-exists and punctures all paradigms of socialization—what reveals the body as that which lies beyond the subject of the signifier and outside the order of symbolic meaning as something that uncannily enjoys repetition insistently and all alone. According to Éric Laurent (2008/2014):

> In Lacan's late teaching, the unconscious is defined as a form of knowledge that acts directly upon the body of the speaking being. It is a break in the representation of the subject within the signifying system. It is a knowledge of incompatibility between the linguistic system and the body's jouissance, a memory of breaking-points, in some sense. The body emerges from this having been fragmented by a host of different trajectories that are stamped with holes. (p. 33)

On the side of the subject, Lacan locates the effects of the signifier and the production of meaning. On the side of speaking-being or *parlêtre*, the effects of the signifier are affects—extra-linguistic effects inscribed on the body and organized around the relation to jouissance. The subject as non-substantial lack of Being is to be contrasted with the body as "enjoying substance" (*la substance jouissante*) (Lacan, 1975/1998, p. 23). Enjoying substance is not to be understood as a given thing that subsequently enjoys itself, but as a thing that is substantial only to the extent that it enjoys, for which enjoyment constitutes not an activity but existence as such. This is not the substantial ego of Freud's "psychical reality," of which Nietzsche was so critical, seeing it as the product of the "four great errors" of metaphysics in the valorization of consciousness and logical causation. On the contrary, enjoying substance reflects Lacan's final attempt to move beyond the ego and the subject (even as lack) in favor of thinking an ongoing process that does not submit itself to but that exceeds the logic of the signifier (presence and absence)—a Real that both "does not stop writing itself" and "does not stop not being written" (p. 59). The Real as enjoying substance is thus another name for what Lacan, also in *Encore*, calls "life," as that which insists beyond Being, desire, meaning, and castration.

Clinical example

A young legal professional (G) came to see me for help dealing with her husband's jealous outbursts and accusations of infidelity. She told me that she had been anorexic as an adolescent, and that the pressure of her husband's unfounded accusations was threatening to drive her back toward this symptom. A twice per week psychotherapy was enough to successfully prevent this from happening. About a year into our work together she began to reconstruct a memory of having been convinced as a child that her parents each separately had real families elsewhere, and that their own marriage was just a game they played to assuage her anxieties. Disturbed by this memory, G asked to begin seeing me four times per week for an analysis.

G said that the idea of more weekly sessions excited her, but the thought of moving to the couch made her anxious. Some weeks into our new schedule, I asked G what kept her from trying the couch. Smiling flirtatiously, she asked, "Aren't couches just for sleeping?" The couch seemed anachronistic, and anyway she liked being able to look at my face while she talked. However, she said, this made her feel conflicted, since she had heard that continuing to sit upright in the chair was a form of "cheating." When I asked what other concerns prevented her from moving to the couch, she repeated how pleasurable it was for her to look at me, and that it would be "weird if you were behind me." When I repeated back to her this chain of signifiers, she immediately registered the impact of her words, appeared mortified, and told me that she had once been taken advantage of sexually while in her late teens. She said that when she had told her husband about this, expecting his sympathy, it had only exacerbated his jealousy over the fact that she would "let" someone else do this to her. She became distraught and began to cry.

When she returned for the next session, G announced that she had fallen deeply in love with me. She worried that her husband might find out about the depth of her feelings for me. She said she had not spoken of her love before because she suffers from the question as to whether I might feel as intensely towards her. "This isn't transference," she insists, "this is real love!" She wonders whether I agree, or if I only see her love for me as a sign of pathology. She says that it feels to her like we are having an affair, and she is frustrated that we only talk, but our talking feels physical: "Why does this feel physical? I don't understand. How does it get this intense? You're all the way across the room, and yet it still feels physical."

Over the ensuing months, G's efforts to seduce me into abandoning the position of analyst dominate the sessions. She says she feels "touched" by me, by my words: "You feel so genuine to me. I wish you could *really* get to know me. You don't get to know me the way I want you to … How can you have this kind of relationship with me, and be so good at staying over there? I feel so enamored with you. Is it just a fantasy, or is this real life? You engage in me—with me!"

Attending to her slip, I say, "I touch you, and I engage *in* you."

"But only verbally ..." she laments. Then, "Why won't you just fuck me? I wish you wanted to know what I'm *really* like. I wish you didn't have so much control, because I have none right now."

She went on to fantasize about crossing the room and sitting on my lap, and what my response would be. Would I anxiously withdraw from her, or would I stay calm? She says she experiences my self-control as an indication of my strength and my confidence in my desirability—qualities she finds lacking in her husband and her father: "I need somebody to tell me what's going to happen next, and that it will be okay. My husband can't do that. My dad can't. My husband is always saying he's a feminist and he believes in equality. I believe in that up to a point, but beyond that point I just get sick of it and I wish he would take charge." She then admitted that she likes it when she is hit on by random men on the street, something she had always told me she hates because it's "objectifying and sexist." Now she says, "I don't completely hate gender disparities. I'm a feminist but not one hundred per cent. I still dress like a woman! It would be nice for someone to take me out once in a while and have some semblance of wanting to take care of me. Am I not supposed to want that? My husband makes me feel bad about it. I don't mind not being equal."

Some weeks later, after describing an upsetting incident at work, G says she had wanted to call me but had stopped herself. Then she says she didn't need to call me because she could handle it, and that she can handle a lot more than she tells me she can: "I devalue myself in a lot of ways. I pretend like I don't know things that I do, or that things are more stressful than they really are. But sometimes, when I don't see you, even if it's just in between sessions, I feel like I'm bleeding."

When I echo the word "bleeding," she seems anxious but offers no associations. She goes on to talk about having to speak French at her job. She does not speak French fluently, but it seems to me that she gets on quite well. When I say, "You don't speak it fluently, but it sounds like you're able to let it flow," again she gets anxious, and she says that before when I highlighted the word "bleeding" she thought I was referring to menstrual bleeding. Now the word "flow" confirms this. I point out that these are her associations, not mine, and I ask her what else comes to mind. She says two things: being pregnant and being anorexic. Being anorexic had stopped her menstrual cycle, which had comforted her. She says she wishes she didn't menstruate, but she's glad that she does because it means she is not pregnant. She tells me that secretly she feels she is not a "proper woman" because, despite what she's told her friends and family, she doesn't have any particular affinity for children.

The next time the topic of her using the couch comes up, G has the thought that the couch will turn the warmth of our relationship into the coldness of a medical procedure. She then spontaneously reports an image of me sitting on her stomach, her abdomen cut open revealing an emptiness inside. She thinks this means she is afraid that I will take something essential away from her. In addition she worries that she is "too much" for me, and that I might suddenly decide at any moment that I can no longer work with her.

* * *

The erotic transference that had evolved in this case illustrates several of the paradoxes that define the clinical experience of transference. These paradoxes appear as a series of interrelated questions that cause the analysand both to suffer and to enjoy: Is this transference, or real love? Fantasy, or real life? How can the verbal feel so physical? How can there be such intimacy between two people who do not—cannot— "really know" each other? Just as she insists on a distinction between transference and "real love" (a distinction that belongs to metaphysics), G struggles to account for the intensity of her feelings by locating their cause or origin in the relation to the analyst as object. As Lacan put it in his *Seminar XI* (1973/1981), "In persuading the other that he has that which may complement us, we assure ourselves of being able to continue to misunderstand precisely what we lack" (p. 133). It is in this sense, and as the work with G demonstrates, that transference functions both as vehicle for the treatment and as obstacle to the cure.

If we approach the case from the perspective of the subject of the unconscious as non-substantial lack of Being, analysis ought to be oriented around persuading the patient to give up on the fantasy of full jouissance—of absolute satisfaction—that she insists on situating in the relationship to the analyst as object. This insistence would be what transference indicates, for Lacan, as the "closing" of the unconscious (1973/1981, p. 130), precluding interpretation and which must be endured silently, without speech from the place of *le mort*. To the extent that he appears as the one who will ultimately fulfill her desire, the analyst is in the position of the Other who can facilitate the patient's acceptance of Symbolic castration, instead of supporting her tortured search for an other who would be capable of filling in her lack of Being where everyone else from her parents to her husband have failed (due to no fault of their own). Relieving the patient of this fantasy would allow new forms of enjoyment to emerge by liberating the subject of the signifier from the inertia of fixed signification.

From the perspective of speaking-being, however, something more is at stake in the material. G's efforts to flood the Other with the Real ("why won't you just fuck me?"), which she fears will provoke me into abandoning her for being "too much," indicates not only her enjoyment in provocation as a remainder produced by language, but an enjoyment that threatens to overwhelm her because it is all too precariously inscribed on her body. This "too much" is the jouissance that she both contains and expresses in her tendency toward anorexia. Rather than serving as a structure of address, what the patient experiences as a result of the analyst's ability to maintain a neutral, interpretive stance is the intensity of her singular, originary encounter with jouissance, the avoidance of which keeps her stuck at the level of Symbolic identity ("I'm anorexic," she told me in our first session, despite not having shown signs of anorexia for almost twenty years—this was an identity that previous therapists had actually encouraged her to assume, to fasten her identity around a particular signifier as something that tells her about what she *is*). What was threatening was not the potential return of her adolescent anorexia, but the return of something that, as it turned out for G (as well as, apparently, for her jealous husband), the signifying system of marriage relations could not contain. What might otherwise have articulated itself self-destructively within the moral framework provided by institutionalized monogamy emerged in the analytic relationship as an erotic transference. G's efforts at seduction are easy to endure without countertransferential anxiety once one realizes that she does not want to sleep with me, rather she wants me to want to sleep with her, that is, to abandon the position of analyst and to be done with this whole business of analysis which brings her so close to her jouissance and to its possible transformation. Seduction is not the truth of her demand. Truth lies rather at the level at which she experiences herself as "touched" by my words—and not in terms of *what* they mean as attempts at communication, but *how* they mean as this is experienced "directly" at the level of the body. Clinically, it is a question of style.

Graciela Brodsky (2014) notes that in his later teaching Lacan recast his earlier statement, "the Real is the impossible" as "the Real is the impossible to bear," and that these are two quite different positions. The

Real as "impossible to bear" is not impossible merely in that it resists symbolization, but in the weight it carries as a bearing on the body, as urgency or as excess. Such excess is what brings a patient to analysis to begin with. With G this was evident in her adolescent anorexia and in the perceived threat of its return under the pressure of her husband's jealousy. In the course of the analysis this impossible to bear was not alleviated but seized upon as the vehicle for transformation. This is the essence of Lacan's later approach: The Symbolic and the Imaginary cannot saturate the Real, cannot prevent the repetitive insistence of the drive beyond desire. The later Lacan comes to situate the repetition of the drive on the side of the vehicle rather than on that of the obstacle.

In speaking, speech tells not *the* truth of experience, but a semblance of truth—what Nietzsche calls a "mask" or "veil," echoing the fragment from Heraclitus, "Nature loves to hide" (Curd, 2011, p. 42). Truth is revealed as no more trustworthy, yet no less potentially effective, than a lie. It was Nietzsche who first introduced this consideration of truth as having "the structure of a fiction" by refusing the metaphysical opposition of truth and untruth. Truth conceived psychoanalytically, for Lacan, is not some grandiose notion of universal or objective truth, but truth assimilated to the particular in the form of a fiction, of becoming, as trace of the impossibility of being All. Lacan thus describes truth non-metaphysically as amenable to change. Truth considered from the perspective of psychoanalysis—that is, from the position of the clinic—is not dogmatic, metaphysical truth. Psychoanalytic truth is always partial and becoming-other than itself, it is not absolute. People enter analysis in a state of not knowing, and with the intention of overcoming this state, wanting to know the truth (cause) as to *why* they are suffering. In the process of looking for this truth, the analysand is given the opportunity instead to rewrite his or her story, not to discover its ultimate meaning, source, or end. There is no fundamental truth at the end of an analysis, but a new construction that emerges from the analyst's efforts to break apart the identification of meaning with Being in the form of fantasy, and to facilitate becoming as drive toward the repetition of difference.

* * *

A year later, having since moved to the couch, and in the process of coming to terms with how uninterested she is in motherhood, G's marriage began to appear to her not unviable but arbitrary, in the sense that she can genuinely love her husband without having to feel trapped by him. What she had feared would destroy her relationship had in fact strengthened it. Surprised at the turns her perspective had taken, she gave an example of just how "non-traditional" she had discovered herself to be. A friend had been chiding her for the fact that she did not bake for her husband. Her husband, she had responded, did not want her to bake for him—after all, he is a feminist. She had never even turned on the oven in their apartment. Out of curiosity, she decided to see what it was like. When she attempted to do so, she discovered that all along it didn't even work. Almost convulsing with laughter, she marveled at the fact that, "It's taken me two years to figure out that my oven is broken! And I couldn't care less!"

Delusions, constructions, perspectives

Almost ten years after having distinguished the discourse of the analyst from the discourse of the university, and on the occasion of the transfer of the Department of Psychoanalysis from Vincennes to the University at Saint-Denis, Lacan returned to the question of the relationship between psychoanalysis and the university, this time in a much shorter text. This brief document is paradoxically a defense of the place of psychoanalysis within the university that argues that the analytic experience is precisely something that cannot be taught. Published in 1979 under the title (not Lacan's own), "There are four discourses," Lacan (1979/2013a) asks, "How does one go about teaching what cannot be taught?" (p. 3). Where psychoanalysis is conceived as a practice of "teaching what cannot be taught," this is intended to situate the clinic beyond all vestiges of the domain of pedagogy. Pedagogy, as a form of authoritarianism, is an inherently metaphysical relation. Pedagogy traffics in idealization, identification, and fantasies of causality: The teacher possesses knowledge that the student lacks. In relating to the teacher, the student is presumed to relate to the cause of knowledge that comes to be installed within himself if he submits himself properly. In principle this framework can be developed into standardized curricula that will eventually require not teachers but administrators. These have been the delusions of pedagogy since Plato's founding of the Academy. For Lacan, non-analytic therapeutic approaches (including most predominant versions of psychoanalysis itself) are based on this same pedagogical strategy. Patients indeed come to analysis looking for just such an authority figure—the kind that the university provides, in the form of the subject-supposed-to-know—but must be disabused of this fantasy by means of an interpretive process. This effort not only lies outside but challenges the very foundations of authoritarianism, and it is why, from a Lacanian perspective, psychoanalysis is inherently inassimilable to what passes today for scientific institutions.

In his commentary on Lacan's short text, Jacques-Alain Miller (2013) emphasizes the extent to which Lacan here disrupts his search for a matheme of psychoanalysis—a formula that would encapsulate what psychoanalysis is, for everyone and for all. Lacan's approach for the greater part of his career had been an attempt to establish psychoanalysis as a science based on the principles of structural linguistics (Saussure) and on the elementary structures of kinship (Lévi-Strauss). In the last decade of his teaching, Lacan gives up on this effort, as well as on efforts to defend the figure of the subject as absence or lack (influenced by Sartre), in favor of a rethinking of the body and its place in the analytic experience as talking cure. According to Lacan, psychoanalysis is a discourse that "excludes domination" in that it "teaches nothing." To the extent that the relationship between analyst and analysand "excludes domination," Lacan asserts, "There is nothing universal about it, which is precisely why it cannot be taught" (1979/2013a, p. 3). The talking cure is not a teaching cure. Analytic experience cannot be taught because it does not have to do with language conceived of as a tool of communication.

Miller also underscores in this context the conjunction of Lacan's claim that psychoanalysis "cannot be taught" with his disarming statement, "everyone is mad": "How does one go about teaching what cannot be taught? This is something Freud ventured into. He thought that all is but a dream and that everyone (if one can say such a thing), that everyone is mad, that is, delusional" (ibid.). According to Miller, Lacan's claim that, "everyone is mad, that is, delusional," is the position statement of a Freudian practice that obviates claims to universality and that attempts to bring to light the singularity of each patient's experience as an experience of "truth." Playing on the French word for truth—verité—Lacan describes truth as varité—variety or multiplicity of truths as what the analytic experience engenders, allowing for new truths to replace old truths. This is the Lacanian concept of cure: not as the removal of symptoms in the service of adaptation, but as providing new symptoms in the place of old symptoms, new forms of satisfaction or ways of being in the place of those that no longer serve their function of providing access to enjoyment without excessive suffering. For Lacan, there is no non-symptomatic subjective position, there are only symptoms that provide more or less access to enjoyment. Subjectivity is intrinsically symptomatic, and analysis is an effort to reconfigure this condition rather than to alleviate it. It is in this sense that, for Lacan, although he does not explicitly align himself in this way, the Freudian concept of the symptom translates Nietzsche's concept of perspective into a clinical register. A science capable of treating the particular rather than the universal in this way would be a science neither positivist nor metaphysical.

Miller treats Lacan's attribution of the statement "that everyone is mad, that is, delusional" to Freud rather illegitimately, as if this summarized Freud's position from the outset, beginning with the approach to dreams as the royal road to the unconscious. In doing so he follows the typical Lacanian procedure of making Freud appear more radical in his thinking than he actually was. Surprisingly, what Miller does not reference is the specific essay in which Freud actually does entertain this very claim, to which Lacan might be referring, and to which Miller had devoted himself in a seminar delivered over a decade earlier. This is Freud's late paper, "Constructions in analysis" (1937d). Miller had provided a detailed commentary on this text to an Italian audience in 1994, and it is a text with which Lacan was certainly familiar. If in the later phase of his teaching Lacan renounces all pretensions to universality in the name of a psychoanalytic practice grounded in an approach to truth as non-objective, conceiving the category of truth otherwise, this means that Lacan is rediscovering the link that Freud as a clinician shared with Nietzsche in its innermost, non-metaphysical dimension. The Lacanian "return to Freud" might in this way shed light on what Nietzsche might have said about psychoanalysis as an experimental-scientific practice.

In "Constructions in analysis," Freud raises the question concerning the relationship between psychoanalysis and the framework that opposes construction and truth, subjectivity and objectivity—the question, as Freud indicates in the essay's opening paragraph, as to what exactly "yes" and "no" mean from a psychoanalytic perspective. This is nothing less than the question concerning the relationship between psychoanalysis and science. At the beginning of the essay Freud invokes a hypothetical interlocutor who charges psychoanalysis with enforcing the principle, "Heads I win, tails you lose." According to this charge, analysts set themselves up always to be right: If the patient says yes, it means yes, the interpretation is correct. If the patient says no, it means yes, the interpretation is correct, but the patient is resisting. This is the inner logic of reversibility, concreteness, positivism, and metaphysics. Freud responds by indicating that the analyst is not interested in whether the analysand responds with "yes" or "no," but in the fact *that she responds*, and in the ways this response either sustains itself or fails to sustain itself. What Freud sees, what his interlocutor (a "certain well-known man of science") has such difficulty grasping, is that the analyst must not have "faith in opposite values" such as those attributable to yes or no, or to the opposition of historical truth and narrative construction. In his "Marginalia to 'Constructions in analysis,'" Miller (1994/2011) notes that the imaginary interlocutor who accuses the analyst of operating according to the principle, "Heads I win, tails you lose," expresses Popper's (1935/2002) argument concerning falsifiability, published just two years earlier. This argument claims to provide an objective formula for determining what is objective (scientific) and what is not, and that is grounded in clear meanings attributable to "yes" and "no," which is precisely what Freud here is at pains to distance himself from. In a clinical context, "yes" and "no" are not definitive answers to categorical questions but individuating-relational responses to dynamic relations of force.

Calling into question the metaphysical opposition between "yes" and "no" quickly leads Freud into all sorts of areas where basic conceptual structures appear on the verge of dissolving: those structures that oppose fact and interpretation, perception and hallucination, neurosis and psychosis, and even psychopathology and psychoanalysis. By the end of the essay, Freud goes so far as to compare the psychotic patient's delusions with the analyst's efforts at construction: "The delusions of patients appear to me to be the equivalents of the constructions which we build up in the course of analytic treatment" (p. 268). Freud had entertained this resemblance as early as the Schreber case (1911c), where he wrote, "It remains for the future to decide whether there is more delusion to my theory than I should like to admit or whether there is more truth in Schreber's delusion than other people may, as yet, be prepared to believe" (p. 75). Commenting on the final section of the "Constructions" paper which concludes with this striking comparison, Miller (1994/2011) writes, "The title of this third section could be: *The delusion as the patient's construction*. But clearly this has a nether side, which is *the construction as the analyst's delusion*" (pp. 50–51, emphases in original). Reason, Freud indicates, is itself always an apparently reasonable interpretation of reality, whereas delusion is an interpretation that appears less than reasonable, though not, of course, to those who are deluded: "If we consider mankind as a whole and substitute for it the single human individual, we discover that it too has developed delusions which are inaccessible to logical criticism and which contradict reality" (1937d, p. 268). To maintain what by the end of the essay has become an all too fluid distinction between reason and delusion, both of which ultimately constitute forceful appeals to immediately unassailable "facts," Freud continues to insist that all mental illness is a suffering from memory—that there is always "a fragment of *historical truth*" (p. 267, emphasis in original) even in the distortions of psychosis—so that all treatment must therefore remain an experience of archaeological remembrance. It is, however, the difference between memory as recall and memory as interpretation that Freud otherwise begins to reconsider. Having spent decades laboring over the question as to whether psychoanalysis essentially concerns historical (objective) or narrative (subjective) truth—whether it is a rigorous science or yet another form of suggestion—Freud appears to indicate that analysts ought not to become too involved in this debate. There is something too insistent—symptomatic, if not delusional—about this opposition itself.

Freud relates the analyst's practice of construction to the production of "ultra-clear" (*überdeutlich*) recollections bordering on hallucination in otherwise neurotic patients. Hallucinations and delusions, he claims, can be observed in both neurosis and psychosis. What makes these experiences symptomatic is, "a belief in their *actual presence* [...] added to their clearness" (p. 266; emphasis added). This is to say that what relates neurosis and psychosis is the tenacity of the symptom as a structure that provides satisfaction by persisting over time, refusing transformation and difference by insisting on the immediate identity of the actual and the present (an identity that metaphysics, on Nietzsche's account, calls Being). Neurotics are "psychotic" to the extent that they remain committed to their symptoms, their delusional interpretations of reality that keep them stuck at the level of avoiding the Real by generating meaning symptomatically. It is for this reason that Lacan declares, "everyone is mad"—not that everyone is psychotic, but that everyone is delusional, to the extent that we experience meaning at all, and in such a way that we are capable of both forming debilitating symptoms and forming ideals worth sacrificing ourselves for.

A symptom is what once made sense, and which persists despite the fact that it no longer makes sense. This is why Lacan insists on the priority of the signifier over signification, on the form that meaning assumes rather than the meaning of meaning itself. What is specific to psychoanalysis as a talking cure is its refusal to argue with the patient about the sense that his symptom does not make. The effort of classical psychoanalysis is to attempt to recall or to reconstruct the context in which what has since become meaninglessly, repetitively symptomatic, once did appear to make sense. This is a form of liberation for Freud: the experience not of seeing that an idea is irrational, but of encountering the historical context from out of which it is generated and within which it appears to be rational, such that the rational and the irrational can be shown to have coincided over time. Amalgamating the rational and the irrational in this way was already Nietzsche's practice of genealogy: a tracing back to origins that does not uncover eternal truth but a contingent, interpretive process of development through which the experience of truth is not revealed but produced. For Nietzsche, truth as factual, positive knowledge is always delusional. It is an interpretation that fails to recognize itself as interpretation, producing a sense of subjectivity as atemporal essence or ground as a defense against the anxiety, uncertainty, and non-knowledge intrinsic to becoming, transformation, and change. Psychosis emerges at the conjunction of knowledge and certainty as an experience of "actual presence"; it has to do not simply with the strangeness of ideational or associative content, but with an inability to call one's experience of that content into question, regardless as to how unusual or seemingly normal it may be. The insistence over time of neurotic symptoms is not unlike the intractable delusions of the psychotic in this sense. Where neurosis is considered to be opposed neither to psychosis nor to normality, but as the general condition of the psyche as a field of irreducible dynamic conflict, the result would be the eradication of all absolute distinctions between pathology and the moral ideal of "mental health." Processes of individuation and the pursuit of this moral ideal are not intrinsically coincident. Thus according to Miller, echoing Lacan, what this ultimately indicates is that one has to be crazy to appear normal in the first place. The experience of "having an inner world" approximates psychosis as a form of intensive delusional commitment. This is what Lacan had always meant by "the subject of the signifier." Enduring subjective identity arbitrarily coalesces around particular signifiers that fix the subject's primordial relation to jouissance such that it is the relation to language—and not identification with others as objects—that gives the necessary illusion of being a cohesive self.

Laughter

In the early phases of his teaching, Lacan had conceived of jouissance as that which makes up for the inability of language fully to represent who or what one is. In the later phase of his teaching he abandons the claim that it is our attachment to meaning that produces jouissance as a remainder that covers over our Being as lack. He arrives instead at a conception of jouissance not as a byproduct of the constitutive subordination of a subject to language, but as that which allows us to enjoy speech originally as self-invention in excess of communication or the production of meaning: speaking-being (*parlêtre*) as becoming or "bespeaking." Speech is not a failure of the attempt at using language to represent oneself to the Other; it is the auto-affective articulation of an enjoyment or enjoying substance that persists even in the absence of any structure of address. This is reflected in the priority Lacan eventually assigns to the drive over desire, departing from his earlier perspective entirely. In replacing concern for desire with concern for the drive, Lacan moves away from the early influence of Hegel and towards a framework more resonant with Nietzsche's thinking. In doing so, he overcomes the intrinsic nihilism of the first decades of his approach to Being as castration or lack, in a way that intersects with Nietzsche's appreciation of the living body as that which ultimately makes no sense but that needs no justification. Affirming this, as the case of Nietzsche indicates, involves risking the possibility of breakdown, over which the transference attempts to hold the patient together and to see through to its end. The alternative would be to remain stuck for a lifetime at the level of fixed signification in the form of a factical status quo that insistently, symptomatically seeks to justify itself as what should appear unquestionably obvious to everyone.

Lacan's abandonment of the category of the subject of the unconscious, in favor of the body as speaking-being or *parlêtre*, is attendant on his efforts to "teach what cannot be taught" in order to "exclude domination." To exclude domination from the clinical relationship—to achieve a scientific status for psychoanalysis by demonstrating that it is not suggestion, unlike so much of what is elevated to the status of science today in the commercial marketplace of contemporary therapeutics—was Lacan's project from the outset of his teaching. He did not always succeed in this effort, but he remained more committed to it than any analyst after Freud. And like the later Freud, Lacan understood that denying the scientificity of psychoanalysis originated in a resistance not just on the part of the interlocutor but at the very heart of the contemporary scientific project itself, to the extent that science today still remains bound to metaphysics—in Lacanian terms: to the logic of the signifier, which endlessly proliferates itself in the binary form of presence and absence, yes and no, which for Nietzsche constitutes the moral framework of right and wrong, the "fundamental faith of the metaphysicians," the "superstitions of logicians." To appreciate the extent to which metaphysics continues to inform the project of modern science requires an experimental practice capable of challenging the enjoyment provided by positivist certainty—the exquisite, bodily ecstasy that produces an authoritarian experience of consciousness in the abstract, reactive form of a *fact* that *knows* it is *right*.

When Lacan asserts that, "everyone is mad," this articulates the central insight of Nietzsche's perspectivism, which is to say the essence of Nietzsche's critique of metaphysics. Perspectivism does not celebrate diversity by condemning the figure of truth, inmixing it with illusion, and asserting the rights of the subjective individual. Rather, perspectivism indicates that what has shaped history are the delusions of the few that have become the realities of the many. Where all values have been revaluated, this is not to say that the delusional structure of all cultural formations is inherently sick, it is rather to assert that those who claim the right to decide what distinguishes sickness from health for everyone and for all do so from a position of *ressentiment*. The distinction between sickness and health cannot be posited as objective or universal, but must be constantly redrawn and experimented upon. Individuation is the ongoing differentiation of "protracted sickness" and health, as of self and world, and with regard to their irreducibly dynamic tension. *Ressentiment*, like jouissance, is exquisitely satisfying in direct proportion to the pervasiveness of the suffering that it engenders. Between them, one cannot clearly assign the values of weakness and strength that had so preoccupied Nietzsche, but when read in conjunction with one another they approximate what Nietzsche had intended to indicate by will to power as the condition of a body that *lives*, what Lacan finally arrived at as a conception of the living body that *enjoys*, and that does so *all alone*. This is not an existential aloneness; it describes rather that, unlike the subject, the body has no correspond-ing object—that its primary relation is to jouissance. There is no end to this enjoyment, this aloneness, but what makes it into a source of suffer-ing is the fact that this endless enjoyment is not something that belongs to the individual but to life itself, as what is capable of continuing on in the absence of any individual living body. For Nietzsche, this must constitute the object of an unconditional affirmation.

The antidote, therefore, to the resentful form of enjoyment that rev-els in conscious facticity is laughter. Laughter issues from the body as the ultimate praise of the particular without concern for the universal, momentarily effacing consciousness and forgetting the weight of the past by invoking a "yes" without "no." It is the increasing inability of what passes for culture today to cultivate laughter that Nietzsche condemns: "On 'the educational establishment'. —In Germany, the higher men lack one great means of education: the laughter of higher men; for in Germany, these do not laugh" (1882/2001, p. 137). To cultivate laughter on the grand scale that is needed today in the face of so much self-destructiveness that oscillates between knowing and not know-ing itself for what it is, one would need the intervention of a joyful—non-metaphysical—science. Does psychoanalysis have something to say about this possibility? According to Lacan, it most certainly does: "The closer we get to psychoanalysis being funny the more it is real psy-choanalysis" (1975/1988, p. 77). But as Nietzsche knew too well, and as Freud and Lacan were both eventually forced to admit, those who are unshakably assured of themselves are all too capable of mocking and dismissing those who challenge their delusions. Such is the inherent strength of weakness when confronted with the inherent weakness of strength. Perhaps, then, the fate of psychoanalysis will be not unlike that of Nietzsche's fabled madman upon having announced the death of God:

> Here the madman fell silent and looked again at his listeners; they too were silent and looked at him disconcertedly. Finally he threw his lantern on the ground so that it broke into pieces and went out. "I come too early", he then said; "my time is not yet ..." (1882/2001, p. 120)

Nietzsche's promise

> To breed an animal that is *entitled to make promises*—is that not precisely the paradoxical task nature has set itself where human beings are concerned? Isn't that the real problem *of* human beings?
>
> —Nietzsche, *On the Genealogy on the Morals*

> Mother, I am stupid.
>
> —Nietzsche's last words

Those who have read slowly will have grasped that I have made a series of promises: promises about what taking the time to read Nietzsche today could open up generally, and promises about the specific consequences of such a reading for the future of psychoanalysis. To make promises always entails asserting that one has the right to do so, and as Nietzsche argued there is no ultimate ground upon which one might justify such an assertion. To promise a future is always to take a risk: that things might work out otherwise, that all efforts have been in vain, that domination and control repeat themselves in the very gesture that calls out in the name of the desire for difference. In so many ways this was the risk that Freud oriented us toward in his attempt to cultivate a science

149

capable of analyzing the phenomenon of transference—of tending to what is radically particular in human experience, rather than merely providing explanations of what appears to be universal. Freud's step beyond metaphysics begins at the moment when he stops insisting that Irma accept his "solution" and he begins to question the very framework that opposes questions and answers.

To move beyond this framework does not mean that one is no longer compelled to continue making promises—promises about what treatment can accomplish, about what is worth investing in by committing to an analysis, and promises about what the analyst's authority consists in. To make such promises is to exercise a certain power. Nietzsche had embraced the word "power" as a way of articulating how attempts at asserting dominance in an interpersonal context are based on an essential powerlessness or "weakness." The desire for authority is the mark of the absence of authority. "Strength" consists in an openness to what is other that cannot be figured in metaphysical, subject/object terms. This openness cannot experience itself as a new ground for forms of absolute certainty, but must instead learn to cultivate an anxiety-provoking experience of not-knowing in the service of facilitating difference, alterity, and transformation. This is what Nietzsche meant by will to power as distinct from the will to factual knowledge of positivist science, and as what tends toward the overcoming of reactive logics of domination, opposition, and indifference.

The ability to resist indifference is essential to the ability to make promises, to create future possibility. This ability is peculiar to human beings, as that being capable of conceiving for itself a future beyond mere survival—a future that might be conceived either as some non-finite, eternal "beyond," or as a material future in which what is human becomes human to the extent that it is capable of rescuing itself from its own deeply rooted tendencies towards self-destruction. Affirming this ability is what distinguishes Nietzsche from his teacher Schopenhauer and from those who continue to promote nihilism as an all-encompassing solution to the catastrophes of the world today (e.g., Benatar, 2006; Brassier, 2007; Ligotti, 2010). What is disturbing in face of the fact that there is no one solution to the difficulties people are confronted with is the fact that there are local, non-dialectical opportunities for individuating-relational self-overcoming, but even these often fall short of their own promises and give rise to new edicts to adapt, to produce, to align oneself with existing institutions rather than to create new ones. Nietzsche provides a model for working with, rather than being hardened and immiserated by, this tendency.

Metaphysics is what programs thought to embrace certainty, solemnity, and opposition. Nietzsche demonstrates that this directive is common to the institutions of academic philosophy, religious mono-theism, and modern technological science. Each is bound to an abstract concept of truth that gathers together and subordinates all particularity and difference as derivative distortions of some singular, eternal origin, cause, or "good." For Nietzsche, objectivity is not a scientific but a moral ideal. What links science and democracy today is this appeal to unifying universal truths, which the global marketplace appropriates as an imperative in order to serve its own ends. Celebrating the homogenizing, economic ideal of diversity over and against the agonistic, anxiety-provoking claims of individuated difference, metaphysics insists that we adapt to the demands of the world as it stands rather than develop new strategies for living otherwise:

> The entire West has lost those instincts out of which institutions grow, out of which the future grows: Perhaps nothing goes so much against the grain of its "modern spirit" as this. One lives for today, one lives very fast—one lives very irresponsibly: It is precisely this which one calls "freedom". That which makes institutions institutions is despised, hated, rejected: Whenever the word "authority" is so much as heard one believes oneself in danger of a new slavery. (Nietzsche, 1968b, p. 105)

Psychoanalysis is not just a technique, it is an institution, and for better or for worse, it is not capable of renouncing this dimension of its project. What psychoanalysis teaches cannot be taught in a traditional way, because it is not theory, not philosophy, not "science" in the sense in which this term is governed by the popular imagination. What it addresses can only appear within the context of its own institution—the clinic—and in such a way that does not lend itself to being appropriated by commercial interest.

From Nietzsche's perspective, there is a profound difference between authority and authoritarianism. This is the irreducible difference between strength and weakness—irreducible because the reductive figure of opposition belongs to a weakness so resentful that it cannot even begin to conceive of an other of itself outside its own narcissistic commitments. To oppose is to express a wish to dominate and to control; to wish to dominate and to control is to have already failed at expressing what Nietzsche had called "power." Power is technical and hierarchical, but it is not universal or administrative. "Will to power" names chance, unpredictability, and otherness as that which the world today is relentlessly driven to—but ultimately cannot—eliminate. In this lies the promise of a future for psychoanalysis.

Such a promise, however, is not a guarantee, and is the subject of tremendous hostility. As a case in point, Christopher Bollas (2015), with the careful thoughtfulness that is consistently characteristic of his work, writes:

> I have been working with schizophrenics since the 1960s. I am sometimes asked about the possible causes of schizophrenia. I do not know the answer to this. To me it is rather like asking what causes the being of human being. Nonetheless a certain theme has emerged in my work: To be a child is to endure a prolonged situation in which the human mind is more complex than the self can ordinarily bear. Our minds—in themselves—produce contents that will be overwhelming. To be successfully normal, then, we rather have to dumb ourselves down.

Adapted from what was at the time a forthcoming book, this statement appeared in an opinion piece Bollas authored for *The New York Times*. Readers were invited to respond. A fair number of respondents praised Bollas for his sensitivity and willingness to work clinically with difficult patients rather than immediately to defer to medication and hospitalization. The greater majority of respondents, however, chastised not only the author but psychoanalysis itself for being clueless with regard to the proper treatment of severe mental illness. A common theme concerned the amount of money readers imagined psychoanalysis costs in comparison with other forms of treatment, with the implication that it is simply too expensive to treat psychic suffering even if an ongoing, open-ended approach would be appropriate. Many respondents (especially those who self-identified as mental health professionals) insisted that any effort to treat schizophrenia other than at the level of its irrefutably biological basis was morally unconscionable given the sophistication of contemporary psychiatric knowledge. Bollas's admission concerning his lack of knowledge as to the ultimate cause of schizophrenia was treated as a refusal to accept the facts.

For his part, Bollas had not actually admitted to a lack of knowledge, but to a certain confusion concerning the orientation of the question itself: "To me it is rather like asking what causes the being of human being." On the surface, and without grasping the historical implications of his statement, Bollas had invoked the tradition of metaphysics: Being has no cause, it is itself cause, origin, or ground, such that human being simply *is* and cannot conceive of itself in its absence. But despite the unpretentiousness of his prose, many readers missed the fact that Bollas's statement did not actually concern the etiological origins of schizophrenia; rather it concerned the attitude of clinicians who seek after underlying causes as providing guidelines for corrective clinical procedures. His suggestion was that the effort to make sense of human experience by looking for underlying causes always encounters intrinsic limitations. For those driven to provide objective explanations in order to justify manualized interventions and standardized treatment plans, these limitations are not intrinsic but temporary conditions that the advance of positivist science is in the process of conquering. The disconnect between Bollas's piece and many of the responses it generated was profound. Faces and vase.

In the paragraph just cited, Bollas's lack of comprehension is generative, not prescriptive: "Nonetheless a certain theme has emerged in my work: To be a child is to endure a prolonged situation in which the human mind is more complex than the self can ordinarily bear." When causal logic breaks down and the irrational asserts itself, we are faced with a conception of mind as constitutively in excess of the experience of self: Mind and self are not identical. Self is an effort to contain the inherent excessiveness of the experience of mind. To say that mind cannot be identified with or contained by the experience of self is to return to the Freudian concept of the unconscious: that mind and consciousness, self, or subjectivity are not mutually reducible. This was Nietzsche's theme before it was expanded upon and developed by Freud. To say that the experience of mind is too complex for the self to bear is implicitly to challenge the connection traditionally assumed between causal logic and the allegedly therapeutic function of objective, factual knowledge. This challenge does not issue from theoretical, logical argumentation; it issues rather from the lived experience of the process of development as the "prolonged situation" which the being of human being "endures." This endurance is "overwhelming," and as such it cannot be quantified, measured, or established objectively, because it gives rise to feverish, symptomatic investments in objectivity, measurement, and quantification in the first place. In a notebook entry dated somewhere between November 1887 and March 1888, Nietzsche (2003) writes:

> It's essential that one makes no mistake about the role of "consciousness": *what developed it* is our *relationship with the "external world"*. [...] [W]hat becomes conscious is subject to causal relations entirely concealed from us—the succession of thoughts, feelings, ideas in consciousness tells us nothing about whether this succession is a causal one: but it gives the *illusion* of being so, in the highest degree. Upon this *illusion we have founded our whole notion of mind, reason, logic*, etc. (none of these exist: they are fictitious syntheses and unities) [...]. (p. 228)

Again, for Nietzsche, consciousness as substantial self-awareness is not an inherent given; it evolves from out of a primitively disorganized, unconscious relationship between mind and world. As Bollas indicates, this relationship gradually coalesces around the figure of the subject or self that contains the overwhelming experience of mind by opposing itself to the "external world." Nietzsche puts "external world" in quotes in order to problematize the opposition of the external and the internal, drawing attention to its electric instability and dynamism. This primary relationality—what Nietzsche called becoming—is "entirely concealed from us"—it is concealed from consciousness as a figure of mind modeled on perception in the form of understanding, and which has access only to the illusion of facticity. For Bollas, as for Nietzsche, becoming—dynamically interpenetrating mind-world—is "overwhelming," traumatic. The evolution of an enduring sense of timeless, self-identical subjectivity is an effective response to this trauma. The illusions of self, reason, and logic are necessary and must be embraced, but it would fall short of a rigorously scientific perspective to regard these as essential causes rather than as contingent effects of the real. The developmental achievement of a stable sense of self is not teleologically determined, nor is it intrinsically morally good. Rather, the development of the self is a defensive reaction to the cruel trauma of life: "To be successfully normal, then, we rather have to dumb ourselves down." Nietzsche, fearing the ultimate historical consequences of this tendency, had called this "intentional stupidity." The clinical practice of psychoanalysis as non-metaphysical science is an effort to resist this tendency and to create other possible futures.

REFERENCES

Babich, B. (1994). *Nietzsche's Philosophy of Science*. Albany, New York: SUNY Press.
Bass, A. (2000). *Difference and Disavowal: The Trauma of Eros*. Stanford, CA: Stanford University Press.
Bass, A. (2006). *Interpretation and Difference: The Strangeness of Care*. Stanford, CA: Stanford University Press.
Bass, A. (2007). The as-if patient and the as-if analyst. *Psychoanalytic Quarterly*, 75: 365–386.
Benatar, D. (2006). *Better Never to Have Been: The Harm of Coming Into Existence*. Oxford: Oxford University Press.
Bion, W. R. (1984a). *Learning from Experience*. London: Karnac (original work published in 1962).
Bion, W. R. (1984b). *Elements of Psycho-Analysis*. London: Karnac (original work published in 1963).
Bollas, C. (2002). *Free Association*. Duxford, Cambridge: Icon.
Bollas, C. (2015). A conversation on the edge of human perception. Available at: http://opinionator.blogs.nytimes.com/author/christopher-bollas/
Brassier, R. (2007). *Nihil Unbound: Enlightenment and Extinction*. New York: Palgrave Macmillan.
Britton, R. (1998). *Belief and imagination: Explorations in psychoanalysis*. London: Routledge.

155

Brodsky, G. (2014). The clinic and the Real. Roger Litten (Trans.). *Hurly-Burly*, *11*: 87–89.

Casement, P. (1985). *Learning from the Patient*. London: Guilford.

Coen, S. (2005). How to play with remote patients. *Journal of the American Psychoanalytic Association, 53*: 881–834.

Curd, P. (Ed.). (2011). *A Presocratics Reader: Selected Fragments and Testimonia. Second Edition*. Indianapolis, In: Hackett.

Deleuze, G. (1983). *Nietzsche and philosophy*. Hugh Tomlinson (Trans.). New York: Columbia University Press (original worked published in 1962).

Deresiewicz, W. (2014). *Excellent Sheep: The Miseducation of the American Elite and the Way to a Meaningful Life*. New York: Free Press.

Derrida, J. (1978). Force and signification. In: *Writing and Difference*. Alan Bass (Trans.). London: Routledge (original work published in 1967), pp. 3–30.

Derrida, J. (2002). Nietzsche and the machine. In: *Negotiations: Interventions and Interviews, 1971–2001*. Elizabeth Rottenberg (Ed.). Stanford, CA: Stanford University Press, pp. 215–256.

Derrida, J. (2009). *The Beast and the Sovereign, Volume I*. Geoffrey Bennington (Trans.). Chicago: University of Chicago Press (original work published 2008).

Deutsch, H. (1942). Some forms of emotional disturbance and their relationship to schizophrenia. *Psychoanalytic Quarterly, 11*: 301–321.

Fink, B. (1995). *The Lacanian Subject: Between Language and Jouissance*. Princeton, NJ: Princeton University Press.

Fink, B. (2004). *Lacan to the Letter: Reading Écrits Closely*. Minneapolis, MN: University of Minnesota Press.

Freedman, N. (1998). Psychoanalysis and symbolization: legacy or heresy? In: *The Modern Freudians: Contemporary Psychoanalytic Technique*. Carolyn Ellman, Stanley Grand, Mark Silvan, & Steven Ellman (Eds.). Northvale, NJ: Jason Aronson.

Freedman, N. & Lavender, J. (2002). On desymbolization: The concept and observations on anorexia and bulimia. *Psychoanalysis and Contemporary Thought, 25*: 165–200.

Freud, S. (1911b). Formulations on the two principles of mental functioning. *S.E., 12*: 218–226. London: Hogarth.

Freud, S. (1911c). Psycho-analytic notes on an autobiographical account of a case of paranoia (dementia paranoids). *S.E., 12*: 1–82. London: Hogarth.

Freud, S. (1914g). Remembering, repeating, working-through. *S.E., 12*: 147–156. London: Hogarth.

Freud, S. (1915e). The unconscious. *S.E., 14*: 166–204. London: Hogarth.

Freud, S. (1937c). Analysis terminable and interminable. *S.E., 23*: 209–253. London: Hogarth.

Freud, S. (1937d). Constructions in analysis. *S.E.*, *18*: 255–269. London: Hogarth.

Grosskurth, P. (1977). *Melanie Klein: Her world and her work*. Northvale, NJ: Jason Aronson.

Heidegger, M. (1968). *What is Called Thinking?* J. Glenn Gray (Trans.). New York: Harper Perennial (original work published 1954).

Heidegger, M. (1991a). *Nietzsche, Volumes One and Two*. David Farrell Krell (Trans.). New York: Harper Collins (original work published in 1961).

Heidegger, M. (1991b). *Nietzsche, Volumes Three and Four*. David Farrell Krell (Trans.). New York: Harper Collins (original work published in 1961).

Heimann, P. (1950). On countertransference. *International Journal of Psychoanalysis*, *31*: 81–84.

Hinman, L. (1974). Nietzsche's philosophy of play. *Philosophy Today*, *18*: 106–124.

Huizinga, J. (1971). *Homo Ludens: A Study of the Play-Element in Culture*. New York: Beacon Press (original work published in 1938).

Husserl, E. (1970). *The Crisis of the European Sciences and Transcendental Phenomenology*. David Carr (Trans.). Evanston, IL: Northwestern University Press (original work published in 1954).

Klein, M. (1986). *The Selected Melanie Klein*. Juliet Mitchell (Ed.). New York: The Free Press.

Klein, M. (2002). *Envy and Gratitude and Other Works 1946–1963*. New York: The Free Press (original work published in 1975).

Kofman, S. (2007). The impossible profession. Patience Moll (Trans.). In: *Selected Writings*. Thomas Albrecht, Georgia Albert, & Elizabeth Rottenberg (Eds.). Stanford, CA: Stanford University Press (original work published in 1983), pp. 56–70.

Kris, A. (1982). *Free Association: Method and Process*. New Haven, CT: Yale University Press.

Lacan, J. (1981). *The Seminar of Jacques Lacan Book XI: The Four Fundamental Concepts of Psychoanalysis*. Alan Sheridan (Trans.). New York: W. W. Norton (original work published in 1973).

Lacan, J. (1988). *The Seminar of Jacques Lacan Book I: Freud's Papers on Technique*. John Forrester (Trans.). New York: W. W. Norton (original work published in 1975).

Lacan, J. (1998). *The Seminar of Jacques Lacan Book XX: Encore*. Bruce Fink (Trans.). New York: W. W. Norton (original work published in 1975).

Lacan, J. (2006). *Écrits*. Bruce Fink (Trans.). New York: W. W. Norton (original work published in 1966).

Lacan, J. (2007). *The Seminar of Jacques Lacan Book XVII: The Other Side of Psychoanalysis*. Russell Grigg (Trans.). New York: W. W. Norton (original work published in 1991).

Lacan, J. (2013a). There are four discourses. Adrian Price & Russell Grigg (Trans.). *Culture/Clinic, 1*: 3–4 (original work published in 1979).

Lacan, J. (2013b). Columbia University: Lecture on the symptom. Adrian Price & Russell Grigg (Trans.). *Culture/Clinic, 1*: 8–16 (original work published in 1976).

Laplanche, J. & Pontalis, J.-B. (1968). Fantasy and the origins of sexuality. *International Journal of Psycho-Analysis, 49*: 1–18.

Lasch, C. (1979). *The Culture of Narcissism: American Life in an Age of Diminishing Expectations.* New York: W. W. Norton.

Lasky, R. (Ed.). (2002). *Symbolization and Desymbolization: Essays in Honor of Norbert Freedman.* London: Karnac.

Laurent, É. (2014). *Lost in Cognition.* Adrian Price (Trans). London: Karnac (original work published in 2008).

Ligotti, T. (2010). *The Conspiracy Against the Human Race.* New York: Hippocampus.

Loewald, H. (1980). *Papers on Psychoanalysis.* New Haven, CT: Yale University Press.

Mawson, C. (2004). Pseudo-free association: The sophisticated analytic patient and "as-if" relating. *British Journal of Psychotherapy, 18*: 509–522.

McDougall, J. (1980). *Plea for a Measure of Abnormality.* New York: International Universities Press.

Miller, J.-A. (2011). Marginalia to "Constructions in analysis". Adrian Price (Trans.). *Psychoanalytical Notebooks, 22*: 47–74 (original work published in 1994).

Miller, J.-A. (2013). Everyone is mad. Adrian Price (Trans.). *Culture/Clinic, 1*: 17–42.

Nehamas, A. (1985). *Nietzsche: Life as Literature.* Cambridge, MA: Harvard University Press.

Nietzsche, F. (1961). *Thus Spoke Zarathustra.* R. J. Hollingdale (Trans). London: Penguin (original work published in 1884).

Nietzsche, F. (1962). *Philosophy in the Tragic Age of the Greeks.* Marianne Cowan (Trans.). Washington, DC: Regnery.

Nietzsche, F. (1968a). *The Will to Power.* Walter Kaufmann & R. J. Hollingdale (Trans.). New York: Vintage.

Nietzsche, F. (1968b). *Twilight of the Idols and The Anti-Christ.* R. J. Hollingdale (Trans). London: Penguin (original works published in 1888).

Nietzsche, F. (1989a). *Beyond Good and Evil: Prelude to a Philosophy of the Future.* Walter Kaufmann (Trans.). New York: Vintage (original work published in 1886).

Nietzsche, F. (1989b). *On the Genealogy of Morals and Ecce Homo.* Walter Kaufmann & R. J. Hollingdale (Trans.). New York: Vintage (original work published in 1887).

Nietzsche, F. (1997a). *Untimely Meditations*. R. J. Hollingdale (Trans.). London: Cambridge (original works published in 1873–1875).

Nietzsche, F. (1997b). *Daybreak: Thoughts on the Prejudices of Morality*. R. J. Hollingdale (Trans.). London: Cambridge (original work published in 1881).

Nietzsche, F. (1999). *The Birth of Tragedy and Other Writings*. Ronald Speirs (Trans.). London: Cambridge (original work published in 1872).

Nietzsche, F. (2001). *The Gay Science*. Josefine Nauckhoff (Trans.). London: Cambridge (original work published in 1882).

Nietzsche, F. (2003). *Writings from the Late Notebooks*. Kate Sturge (Trans.). London: Cambridge.

Ogden, T. (1986). *The Matrix of the Mind*. Northvale, NJ: Jason Aronson.

Ogden, T. (1989). *The Primitive Edge of Experience*. Northvale, NJ: Jason Aronson.

Popper, K. (2002). *The Logic of Scientific Discovery*. London: Routledge (original work published in 1935).

Renik, O. (1993). Analytic interaction: conceptualizing technique in light of the analyst's irreducible subjectivity. *Psychoanalytic Quarterly, 62*: 553–571.

Riesenberg Malcolm, R. (1992). As-if: the phenomenon of not learning. In: *Clinical Lectures on Klein and Bion*. Robin Anderson (Ed.). London: Routledge, pp. 114–125.

Rodman, F. R. (2003). *Winnicott: Life and Work*. Cambridge, MA: Perseus Publishing.

Ronell, A. (2002). *Stupidity*. Chicago: University of Illinois Press.

Rose, J. (2000). Symbols and their function in managing the anxiety of change: an intersubjective approach. *International Journal of Psychoanalysis, 81*: 453–470.

Rosegrant, J. (2005). The therapeutic effects of the free-associative state of consciousness. *Psychoanalytic Quarterly, 74*: 737–766.

Roshco, M. (1967). Perception, denial, and depersonalization. *Journal of the American Psychoanalytic Association, 15*: 243–260.

Ross, N. (1967). The "as if" concept. *Journal of the American Psychoanalytic Association, 15*: 59–82.

Safranski, R. (2003). *Nietzsche: An Intellectual Biography*. Shelley Frisch (Trans.). New York: W. W. Norton (original work published 2000).

Sanville, J. (1991). *The Playground of Psychoanalytic Therapy*. Hillsdale, NJ: Analytic Press.

Schrift, A. (1990). *Nietzsche and the Question of Interpretation: Between Hermeneutics and Deconstruction*. London: Routledge.

Segal, H. (1994). Phantasy and reality. *International Journal of Psycho-Analysis, 75*: 395–401.

Steingart, I. (1983). *Pathological Play in Borderline and Narcissistic Personalities.* New York: Spectrum.

Stiegler, B. (2013). *Uncontrollable Societies of Disaffected Individuals.* Daniel Ross (Trans.). Malden, MA: Polity (original work published in 2006).

Stiegler, B. (2015). *States of Shock: Stupidity and Knowledge in the 21st Century.* Daniel Ross (Trans.). Malden, MA: Polity (original work published in 2012).

Strong, T. (1975). *Friedrich Nietzsche and the Politics of Transfiguration.* Chicago: University of Illinois Press.

Tarr, B. dir. (2011). *The Turin Horse.*

Thoreau, H. D. (2003). *Walden.* New York: Barnes and Noble Books (original work published in 1854).

Vattimo, G. (2006). *Dialogue with Nietzsche.* William McQuaig (Trans.). New York: Columbia University Press (original work published in 2000).

Winchester, J. (1994). *Nietzsche's Aesthetic Turn: Reading Nietzsche after Heidegger, Deleuze, Derrida.* New York: SUNY Press.

Winnicott, D. W. (1949). Hate in the counter-transference. *International Journal of Psycho-Analysis, 30*: 69–74.

Winnicott, D. W. (1960). The theory of the parent–infant relationship. *International Journal of Psycho-Analysis, 41*: 585–595.

Winnicott, D. W. (1971). *Playing and Reality.* New York: Routledge.

Zupančič, A. (2003). *The Shortest Shadow: Nietzsche's Philosophy of the Two.* Cambridge, MA: MIT Press.

INDEX

adaptation, 8, 11, 16, 38, 45, 47, 53, 55,
    57, 69, 129, 141
agency, 17, 28, 88, 104
    psychic, 128
    subjective, 40, 121
anti-Semitism, 49, 51, 124
Aristotle, 29, 97, 106
Attention Deficit Disorder, 43
authoritarianism, 90, 112–113, 131,
    140–141, 147, 150–151
autonomy, 48, 82, 84, 89, 103, 128

Babich, Babette, 4–5
Balint, Michael, 62
Bass, Alan, 61–64, 76
becoming, 18–20, 35, 38–39, 51,
    53–54, 58, 61, 68, 76, 86,
    96–101, 106, 117–118, 131,
    139, 145–146, 154
Being, 6, 12, 18–20, 48, 51, 54, 58,
    97–100, 103–106, 116, 126,

129–134, 137, 139, 144, 146,
    152–154
Benatar, David, 150
Bion, Wilfred, 21, 53–57, 63–64, 76,
    109
    contact barrier, 56, 64
    Elements of Psycho-Analysis, 54
    reversible perspective, 54, 56–58,
        63, 67, 76
Bollas, Christopher, 107, 152–154
Brassier, Ray, 150
Britton, Ronald, 84–86
Brodsky, Graciela, 138

Casement, Patrick, 21
castration, 63, 130, 132, 134, 137, 146
causality, 12–13, 26, 28–29, 54, 82, 87,
    100, 134, 140
chance, 11, 13, 15, 20, 54, 73, 94,
    152
Chomsky, Noam, 49, 60